CHILDREN AND HANDEDNESS

MAKING THE RIGHT CHOICES

HUMAN ANATOMY AND PHYSIOLOGY

Additional books in this series can be found on Nova's website
under the Series tab.

Additional E-books in this series can be found on Nova's website
under the E-book tab.

PEDIATRICS - LABORATORY AND CLINICAL RESEARCH

Additional books in this series can be found on Nova's website
under the Series tab.

Additional E-books in this series can be found on Nova's website
under the E-book tab.

HUMAN ANATOMY AND PHYSIOLOGY

CHILDREN AND HANDEDNESS

MAKING THE RIGHT CHOICES

Dr. Geoffrey K. Platt
Dr. Mohsen Shafizadeh
Gordon Revolta

Nova Science Publishers, Inc.
New York

NOTICE TO THE READER

LIBRARY OF CONGRESS CATALOGING-IN-PUBLICATION DATA

ISBN 978-1-61942-226-1

Published by Nova Science Publishers, Inc. † *New York*

CONTENTS

ACKNOWLEDGMENTS

The authors would like to express their appreciation for the assistance that they have been given by:

Mr John de Courcy, Dr Martine Verheul and Mr Mark Sanderson, who are all staff in the Institute of Sport, Physical Education & Health Sciences (SPEHS) at the University of Edinburgh in Scotland and who provided excellent advice and guidance throughout this project.

Mr Charles Revolta and Mr George Byng for their invaluable assistance with the proofreading for this book and without whose help there would be so many errors!

Mr Darren Holloway and Mrs Signa Ashdown for their outstanding work on the best of the photography in the book (the rest was done by the authors!)

To my daughter Ella Platt for her advice on the sections of the book relating to genetics.

The Principals and staff of the following schools:
Abbeyhill Primary School in Edinburgh, Scotland;
Preston Street Primary School in Edinburgh, Scotland;
Oval Primary School in Croydon, London, England;
Gresham Primary School in Croydon. London, England;
who allowed us work with their pupils in the research on which this book is largely based.

To University College London Day Nursery for all their valuable assistance in providing the young models for some of the photography in this book. In particular to Kate Burtenshaw (manager), and staff members Anna Wright, Lisa Carbery, Shully Begum-Miah, Robert Connolly, Louise Paul, Rachel Byam, Stacey Nazarjuk, Bianca Platt, Jo McCormick and Rafael Bihun.

Chapter 1

INTRODUCTION

Handedness has long interested us. We are fascinated by people who live alongside us in the same community and who look the same as us and yet who behave in a way that is fundamentally different to us. This has been reflected in our attitudes to race, creed, color and culture and often it has taken legislation to change these attitudes.

For many centuries infants have been divided in the first years of their lives, into right handed and left handed and being left handed was seen as a problem. It was believed to negatively affect our health, wellbeing, moral standing, intellect, and skills. It is no wonder that parents identifying the first evidence that a child was left handed started to panic, to seek help and to purchase books on the subject to see what could be done. They also sought ways to correct the "problem" by "persuading" the child to use his or her right hand instead.

These attitudes have generated a great deal of research into handedness. This has looked at the causes of left handedness, its effects on those "afflicted" and at potential "cures". In order to do this the research has sought out the problems or conditions that are positively correlated to left handedness. These include:

- "Brain damage;
- Epilepsy
- Reading disability
- Neuroticism
- Alcoholism
- Drug abuse
- Homosexuality
- Aggression
- Criminality
- Mental retardation
- Allergies
- Autoimmune disorders
- Migraines
- Emotionality
- Birth stress
- Chromosomal damage
- Poor spatial ability
- Poor verbal ability
- School failure
- Attempted suicide
- Autism
- Psychosis
- Vegetarianism
- Sleep difficulty
- Slow maturation"

(Coren, 1990, pp. 6-7)

Research has, however, shown us that there is no problem in displaying a strong preference for using either the right or left hand, but that each group possesses a different set of skills and abilities, (which will be looked at later) and that an individual is just as likely to achieve success in life whichever hand he or she prefers to use.

It has, however, also shown us that there are many people, perhaps as high as 25% of the population, who have no strong preference for either hand. These people are called Mixed Handed.

Definitions

Mixed Handed. These are people who display no strong preference for either their right or left hand, who may use either hand to undertake a specific task, who may use different hands to undertake different tasks or who swap hands more than occasionally when undertaking a task. The group includes those who are ambidextrous and those who are ambivalent.

Ambidextrous. This means that they are of, or above, average ability and skill in both hands.

Ambivalent. These people are uncertain which hand to use and frequently lack ability and skill in either hand and exacerbate this by failing to decide a preference and therefore fail to consistently practice and improve the skill and ability of the chosen hand.

It is this ambivalent group that experience difficulties, particularly if rushed or pressured to select a preference and who can then suffer consequences, sometimes serious ones. These are the children for whom this book is written.

Recent social changes

For almost as long as anybody can remember, children attending school for the first day of their education, whether aged four and a half years, as in the United Kingdom, or aged six years, as in the United States, have always known whether they prefer holding a pen, pencil or crayon in their right or left hand.

This has allowed primary school teachers to arrange exercises in coloring, tracing, drawing or writing, confident that the children will pick up the pencil or crayon and simply proceed. The teacher can then go around the class praising the children, exhorting them to try harder and issuing advice where necessary.

It is not that children always have an innate knowledge of whether they are right or left handed, but that long hours spent sitting with parents, usually mothers, practicing holding a crayon or coloring pencil, scribbling, securing parental attention, receiving parental praise and simply having fun and creating "artworks" that were valued, have encouraged them to "think" unconsciously about whether they preferred using their right or left hand and whether they performed better using their right or left hand.

If, for any reason, parents were unavailable there was usually a steady and constant supply of grandparents or uncles and aunts from the wider family ready and willing to step into the void.

This all meant that by the time that the children reached the age of six years they had selected their preferred hand and that teachers did not have to worry and could expect every child to know whether they held a pencil in their right or left hand and be able to move forward to coloring, tracing, drawing and writing.

But society changes continuously and so does its standards. Young people are writing less frequently than previously. Teenagers are more likely to send text messages or emails. They have designed their own spelling for text messages. They have designed a way of using "double thumbs" to input text into a mobile 'phone. Letter writing is seen as a Victorian skill that is no longer required. Many schools have identified writing as superfluous in the current technological age and are replacing writing lessons with keyboarding lessons.

A team of researchers that recently visited a local school were very surprised to find ALL thirty members of the class, average age of four and a half years, and in their first week of full-time education, using a double thumbs technique when asked to input a number to a mobile 'phone. Clearly they had been watching their parents closely and were now imitating what they had seen them doing.

In many families, particularly in the current financial crisis, both parents are called upon to work in order to maintain the desired standard of living. In many other families, there is only one parent, either because the parents never got married or because they have become divorced or separated. In all these circumstances, there is less time for parents to devote to raising children. Unfortunately, in many cases the wider family has often also been lost as the need to travel for employment and housing prevents daily or even weekly contact.

Many parents will protest at this generalization and proclaim the number of hours that they spend with their child, but whilst parents and children often spend time together, they are often not bound together in some joint venture, the child is not the center of the adult's attention and the parent is having to fulfill some other obligation. This was recently brought home by a story that was told by a local school principal.

A Personal Anecdote

"I live in an area with some of the largest and most expensive houses in the country. In most families both parents work and frequently they have to work very long hours to pay for their chosen lifestyle.

There is a school just up the road. One of the 5 year old children was injured at school and received a 4 inch cut right across his forehead. It looked terrible, but was actually only a scratch. The Principal realized that it was too late to call the mother to the school as it was only 20 minutes until the children were due to go home normally. The Principal decided to keep the child with her until she met the mother and was able to explain to her what had happened.

The mother was a little late arriving at school and another mother engaged the Principal in conversation, so that the Principal missed seeing the mother of the injured child. The mother took the injured child and put him in the car, a large Range Rover. She strapped the child into the car. They drove to the supermarket and she unstrapped the child and took him to the supermarket. She strapped the child into the trolley and walked around the supermarket. When they finished, the mother took the child out of the trolley and strapped him back into the car.

The mother and child talked about the days that they had had and about what they were having for tea and other items of mutual interest. Mother was pleased that she had been able to have this time with her son as it was not always possible.

At 7.00 p.m. the father of the injured child came home and was surprised to see the large cut across his forehead. Mother had to admit that she had not previously noticed it and that she knew nothing about it. In the four hours that mother and child had spent together, she had not made eye contact with the child as she struggled to complete the required household tasks in the time available.

Parents are working at keeping house, working at jobs etc., but do they ever really SEE the child? This is why the children cannot control their movements or know if they are right or left handed."

Since 2007/8 teachers of Reception Classes (where children go in their first year at school) have suddenly reported that around 25% of their children are arriving at school without knowing whether they prefer to hold crayons or pencils in their right or left hand. When the teachers pass around a block of paper and a box of crayons and announce a simple coloring task, they are met with a sea of blank faces, whose owners do not know how to hold a crayon or pencil, or which hand to put it in. The teachers, in turn, have never been taught how to identify whether a child is right or left handed. They do not have time to spend with each child individually tutoring them in how to hold a pencil and whether they are right or left handed. This must cause blind panic in a young teacher.

This situation has resulted in over 300 teachers in the United Kingdom writing to the teacher's journal, the "Times Educational Supplement", pleading for guidance. This is, by far, the largest number of teachers seeking advice on any topic in education and prompted the authors to undertake a large research project and to write this book.

Traditional roles associated with the two hemispheres of the brain

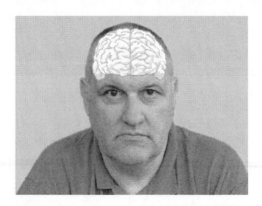

The right hemisphere (left hand control) controls the following functions:

- **Movement in left side of the body;**
- Art;
- Attention;
- Creativity;
- Emotion;
- Inspiration;
- Intuition;
- Language;
- Musical aptitude;
- Perception;
- Pitch and intonation;
- Spatial awareness;
- Synthesis Visual concepts.

The left hemisphere (right hand control) controls the following functions:

- **Movement in right side of the body;**
- Analytical thought;
- Complex rhythm;
- Language;
- Linearity;
- Lists;
- Logic;
- Mathematics;
- Science;
- Sequence;
- Speech;
- Writing

Figure1-1- Traditional roles associated with the two hemispheres of the brain.

Language

Our use of language reveals a great deal about the way that we think about an issue. A good example of this is a philosophical note, dated 1686, which described left handedness as a "digression or aberration from the way which nature generally intended" (In Wile, 1934, p92). Clearly, the original author feels little empathy for those that he considers to be afflicted.

In 1913, Brewster did not mince his words when reviewing the trait of left handedness. He said, "A sound and capable stock, like a right handed one, breeds true generation after generation. Then something slips a cog and there appears a left handed child, a black sheep or an imbecile (p.183).

He goes on "An adult brain, wrecked on the education side, by accident or disease, commonly never learns to do its work on the other, the victim remains crippled for the rest of his days. But a child in whom the thinking area on the other side is still uncultivated, hurt on one side can usually start all over again with the other. A shift of this sort usually carries the body with it, and the child, instead of being permanently disabled, becomes left handed (p179).

Throughout history there is a consistent flow of similar language reflecting similar views, so much that it is impossible to cite them all. These views have persisted across all races, colors, creeds and even political groups, with no kind words surviving to the present and probably never existing.

Although currently considered unacceptable, some of the words used to describe those who have displayed a preference for their left hand over the centuries have included:

In French, "gauche" means both left and clumsy, clearly associating the former with the latter.

In English, "gawky" is the slang equivalent of gauche.

In German, "links" means left, but is often corrupted to "linkisch" meaning clumsy.

In English, "left" comes from the Celtic "lyft" meaning weak or broken.

In Spanish, the idiom "no sur zurdo" has come to mean "to be very clever", but literally translated means "not to be left handed".

In Italian, "mancino" not only means left handed man, it also means a dishonest man.

In Australia, the slang for left handers is "molly-dooker", where duke or dook refers to hand and molly refers to an effeminate man.

In Latin, the word for left is "sinistra" and includes the same association as the English word sinister, to being evil.

Looking for clues in religion

Searching to understand the reasons for the strong feelings against those who are left handed, the researchers investigated attitudes amongst the main religions of the World, Christianity, Islam and Judaism.

Christianity

Wile (1934) reports that the Bible contains eighty positive references to the right hand, each according to it honors, virtues and powers but goes on to say that "there is not one honorable reference to the left hand." James T. DeKay (1997) investigated the Bible further to find one hundred negative references to left handers in it and notes that it refers to those in favor as the "Righteous".

It is interesting, however, that the Bible also contains possibly the only positive reference to left handers prior to World War 2, when, in Judges (20, 16) it records that during the formation of a 700 strong regiment of stone throwers a need for accuracy among them was identified and only left handers were selected, "each of whom could sling a stone at a hair and not miss". Clearly there are advantages and disadvantages in being either right or left handed!

Islam and Hinduism

Many cultures, particularly in the Middle East and Asia, where Islam and Hinduism are centered, have resolved that there should be a "clean" side of the body as well as an "unclean" side, so that eating and greeting friends is done with the right hand and cleaning up after oneself is done with the left hand, which is then kept out of the way to prevent contaminating friends and relatives. These roles are fixed across the community, recognized by the church and do not vary for individual preferences.

Judaism

In the Old Testament (Leviticus 21: 17-21) the rules for selecting priests to perform sacraments in the Holy Temple are described and it goes on to describe the defects and blemishes that disqualify a man from this role (women were not considered for the role). This is discussed further in the Talmud, a set of rabbinical commentaries on Biblical matters, which specifically excludes those who are left handed.

Looking for clues in history

Several researchers have examined evidence from history, such as works of art, some early enough to be painted on cave walls, and the design of some of the earliest tools found thus far, and found evidence that both right and left handers have existed through history.

Looking for clues in animals

In an attempt to understand handedness, without the results being affected by any cultural effects, research has been carried out in:

- Cats (Cole, 1955);
- Mice (Collins, 1969);
- Rats (Pense, 2002);
- Chimpanzees (in captivity)(Finch, 1941);
- Chimpanzees (in wild) (Marchant and McGrew, 1996);
- Gorillas (in captivity) (Annett and Annett, 1991);
- Gorilla (in wild) (Byrne and Byrne, 1991).

Each group contains those with a right hand preference and those with a left hand preference and a majority with a mixed hand use. Two points arise from this research:

1. The number preferring to use their right hand in animals is far lower than in humans
2. The number with mixed hand use if far higher in humans.

Switching

Switching is the process by which a right handed person changes so as to use their left hand, but more frequently where a left handed person changes to use their right hand. It is a vital skill as has been brought home to us all recently with the substantial number of amputees returning home from the Gulf War and Afghanistan. But there have always been people who have suffered injuries in battle or in accidents and who have had to switch hands, ranging from Lord Nelson, the British Admiral from the Battle of Trafalgar, to the American Presidential Candidate, Bob Dole, who both lost the use of their right arm whilst engaging in combat on behalf of their country.

One of the best explanations of the attitudes to left handedness and the pressure brought to bear on left handed students to use their right hands, is set out by Benjamin Franklin, the American statesman, polymath and left hander, in his treatise, "A Petition of the Left Hand" written in the early 1700's. He says, "…but if by chance I touched a pencil, pen or a needle, I was bitterly rebuked; and more than once I have been beaten for being awkward and wanting a graceful manner."

Around 1900, it was recorded that it was policy to tie a child's left hand behind his or her back or strike him or her across the knuckles if he or she was found to be writing with the left hand. The author of this book is able to stipulate that, in one school at least, (the one that he attended!) this conduct persisted until the 1970s.

The pressure to switch does not, however, have to be as obvious as tying children up or beating them. It can be achieved discretely and sometimes, even without the knowledge of the person applying the pressure for change knowing that they are doing it.

As part of the research on which this book is based, in 2010, the authors visited a school in South London. They assessed the members of a Reception Class of 100 children in a school. The children were all aged between 4.5 and 5 years and in the first week of their formal education, yet every one of them claimed to be right handed and every one of them used pens and pencils in their right hands.

As stated previously, approximately 11% of people are generally found to be left handed and to find that not one child was left handed in a group of 100 children was exceptional. When the class teacher was interviewed, she was unable to explain the phenomenon, but agreed that, to the best of her knowledge, none of the children were left handed.

Subsequent observation of the class, not perhaps the best research method, indicated that pens and pencils were always laid out on the right side of the desk and that when assistance was given to any child by demonstrating or correcting, the pen and pencil was always returned to the child's right hand. Similarly, the teacher and her assistant were both right handed and always used their right hand when demonstrating to the class. This gentle pressure appears to have been enough in only one week, to have brought about even a temporary change in the children's behavior and attitudes.

Historically, in at least some cultures, meal times were formal occasions and in the Western culture, among people of a higher class, often the only time that parents and children met during the day. There is evidence that children who attempted to eat with their left hands were strictly admonished and, if they persisted, were denied food until they ate it with their right hand.

David Major, a professor of Education at Ohio State University, undertook a research project that would not receive ethical approval today as it would raise concerns for the wellbeing of the child subject. Professor Major observed his own son from the age of three months to twelve months as he experimented with using both his right and left hands to undertake the usual tasks of infant life. Only when the child reached twelve months did he start to display a preference for one hand and it was the left hand and this preference developed quickly into a strong preference by the thirteenth month.

It was at this stage that the Professor intervened. Attempts to grasp items with the child's left hand were obstructed. When items were requested they were supplied to the right hand, so that by fifteen months the child could be described as right handed and remained so until the study ended at the age of 44 months. Clearly, in this study, which cannot be repeated for the ethical reasons set out above, it did not take long, just two months, to switch the child's preference. (Major, 1906)

Fifty years ago there was a very efficient method of resolving the odd problem in this area. The teacher simply took a few extra belts to school. It is far easier to manage a class where all the children use the same hand, and as all the boys wore shorts held up with a belt and the girls wore dresses tied at the waist with a belt, it was easy to tie the left hand behind the child's back by putting the belt around the left wrist and tying it to the belt holding the clothing. Then the child had to use his or her right hand.

Today, this method is universally considered to be unacceptable. Teachers employing such techniques will be swiftly summoned to see the Principal for sharp advice and if the techniques are continued disciplinary or even criminal prosecution could be considered. There are, however, other techniques that are more subtle, but which can lead to the same result. Some are so subtle that even the teachers that employ them are unaware of what they are doing.

Summary

Three keys facts have been established and are irrefutable:

1. No tribe or culture has ever been found which does not contain at least some left handers;(Perelle and Ehrman, 1994)
2. Every tribe and society possesses a majority of people who prefer to use their right hand (Annett, 2001);
3. The percentage of people who prefer to use their left hand varies from 1% (Hecaen & Ajuriaguerra, 1964) to 40% (Starosta, 2004);

It has been estimated that:

- 64% of children are right handed;
- 11% of children are left handed;
- 25% of children are either ambidextrous or ambivalent.

(Annett, 2001)

Most children, possibly as many as 75%, quickly identify a strong preference for one of their hands that will persist throughout their life. They will consistently use the same hand to write, reach, grab, point and manipulate.

Most of these children will favor the same side for foot as for hand, so that they kick a ball with the right foot if they write with their right hand or they kick a ball with the left foot if they write with their left hand. Similarly, these children will favor the same side for eye as for hand, so that they shoot with the right eye open if they write with their right hand or they shoot with the left eye open if they write with their left hand.

These children will experience few problems with Handedness and will enjoy similar success, whether right handed or left handed, although their skills sets will vary according to their preference (see Figure 1-1).

Some children experience difficulties in identifying a preference and need to give the matter some consideration. It is important that they are allowed time, attention and support to do this without any influence, conscious or unconscious, being exerted upon them.

These children should be encouraged to practice scribbling, drawing, coloring, tracing and writing. They should be praised when they do well and encouraged when things go badly. Their choice of hands should be respected. When demonstrating try to include some demonstrations using your left hand, at least for some of the more simple tasks as this shows an openness to the use of the left hand.

Most importantly, if you are coaching your child and you "borrow" an implement from them, note which hand you take it from and ensure that you return it to the same hand. Constantly taking an implement from their left hand and returning it to their right hand will eventually send a message and apply a pressure to him or her to use his or her right hand.

Chapter 2

WHAT IS IT THAT DECIDES IF WE ARE RIGHT OR LEFT HANDED?

?

Introduction

Each person has two hands, with opposing thumbs, capable of an exceptional range of manual tasks. The hands that in ancient times were used to hunt animals, fish and birds and to gather fruits and vegetables are the same hands that we use today to operate mobile telephones and laptop computers, despite the differing skills that these tasks require.

At first glance, it would appear that people undertake most tasks by using both hands roughly equally and interchangeably, but upon closer inspection it is clear that this is not the case and that each person uses his or her two hands differently. It quickly becomes evident that each of us is stronger in one hand than in the other, that each of us is more skilled in one hand than in the other and that we actually prefer using one hand rather than the other.

Further observation reveals that the strength, skill and preference may vary from task to task. It is not impossible that a man who always writes with his right hand may prefer to kick a football with his left foot. Clearly, each person assesses his or her strength, skill and preference on a task by task basis.

Researchers who have investigated a wide range of cultures and religions state that they have never found a society which did not contain at least some people who preferred their right hand as well as some people who prefer their left hand, although the number that prefer their right hand has always exceeded the number that prefer their left hand (Annett, 2001; Hecaen & Ajuriaguerra, 1964).

Why are the two hands different?

In his influential 1859 book, *"On the Origin of Species"*, Charles Darwin introduced his Theory of Natural Selection and explained that all creatures need to adapt in order to survive. Our ancestors faced a wide range of competitors, predators and potential dangers and needed to react swiftly in order to survive. This involved one dominant hand being "hot-wired" to the brain and maintaining a constant link to it, thereby maximizing its performance. In this way our ancestors were able to react quickly to emergencies and defend themselves against an attack.

Today, this system continues to have value, by allowing us to snatch at a handrail when falling from a bus or to swiftly raise our arm to defend ourselves against a blow directed to the head, etc. The non-dominant hand is only directly connected to the brain when required to undertake some task. It is then disconnected until it is required again. In this chapter we examine the scientific research related to handedness. Firstly, the association between handedness and brain will be discussed, then the development of handedness will be explained, and finally the causes and origins for handedness in human will be described.

So are left handers just freaks?

Some scientists have assessed the number of people who have a preference for their left hand and stipulated these as a percentage of society as a whole. Their assessments have varied between 1% (Hecaen & Ajuriaguerra, 1964) and 40 % (Starosta, 2004), a very wide range, although it is not surprising that the percentage has been found to vary from generation to generation and from culture to culture (Perelle & Ehrman, 1994).

If each person lived in isolation as a hermit, unaffected by social and cultural pressures, it is possible that the number of people with a preference for their left hand may reach as high as 40% and, unable to find large numbers of hermits prepared to participate in scientific research, many scientists have opted to observe animals, such as cats, mice, rats and more recently chimpanzees and gorillas, both in captivity and in the wild, to see what preference they display.

The attitudes to left handed people set out in the first chapter, which resulted in them being universally considered to be freaks, deviants, sinners and criminals is likely to have been the most powerful pressure possible for an individual reviewing his or her strengths, skills and preferences to look favorably on his or her left hand, so as to reduce the percentage of the population with a left hand preference to just 1% of the population.

Currently, the best estimate of hand preference in the U.S and the U.K. is that:

- 64% of children are right handed;
- 11% of children are left handed;
- 25% of children are mixed handed (which includes those who are either ambidextrous or ambivalent).

(Annett, 2001)

In our enlightened times, the problem is not whether a person is right or left handed as their achievements are likely to be of the same order which ever hand they prefer. The children who may have a problem are those who have no strong preference and those who are being pressured to choose their right hand.

What pressure is there on left handers?

Even the most liberal, modern parent today possesses a house full of tools that will apply a quiet, gentle pressure on their children to use their right hand.

From scissors, tin openers, rulers, knives and keyboards, many everyday items are specifically designed to be used by right handed people. Try to purchase a pair of left handed scissors and think back before the internet and Yellow Pages and realize the pressure that, until recently, this put on young people.

When parents and teachers are helping young children to write, the adult will usually demonstrate the skill and allow the child to copy. The adult will usually be a member of the majority right handed set and demonstrate the skill right handedly. If the child makes a mistake the adult will take the implement from the child and correct it. He or she will often, unthinkingly return the implement to the child's right hand. All this applies gentle pressure, but it has been shown that even after a week or two of this type of behavior the child may change his or her preference in order to "fit-in".

Written testimony exists which shows that until the end of World War 2 it was common practice to restrain children from using their left hands. Often belts were used to tie the left hand behind the back. Those who attempted to resist or defy the teacher would receive corporal punishment. The author will specify that this behavior continued in at least one school until the 1970s! Evidence exists that in Germany, which still considers itself to be a disciplined society, these behaviors persist to the present day.

Another technique designed to discourage children from left handedness was the withdrawal of food if the child tried to use his or her left hand to eat it. Possibly the strongest weapon against left handers was the universal view at that time, that left handers were freaks, deviants, sinners and criminals.

The Way that Hand Preference Works

The brain controls all human movement, with the exception of reflexes. The method of connecting the two hands to the brain is different, according to whether the hand is the dominant hand or not. The dominant hand is "hot-wired" to the brain and maintains a constant link to it. In this way it is able to react quickly to all emergencies by defending the person against any attack, to snatch at a handrail when falling from a bus, etc. The non-dominant hand is only directly connected to the brain when required to undertake some task. It is then disconnected until it is required again.

An Example

If I want to drink a sealed bottle of a fizzy drink, I will pick it up with my dominant hand and put it down in front of me. I then take hold of the bottle with my non-dominant hand, whilst I pick up the bottle opener in my dominant hand and wrench off the sealed cap. I then put down the bottle opener and pass the bottle from my non-dominant hand to my dominant hand in order to put the bottle to my mouth to drink.

The non-dominant hand, in other words, was "woken up" to do a job and then went back to "sleep" when the dominant hand could manage on its own.

We tend to think that we have one preferred hand that we use to undertake all tasks and another hand that we simply bring into play when we require a second hand in order to complete a task, but this is not quite true. The range of factors that influence the selection of hands to undertake a task, include skill, previous experience and hand preference.

In the previous chapter we looked at the division of tasks undertaken by the right and left hemispheres of the brain and when undertaking a new task we tend to consider which hand is likely to be best suited to the task before we even start working. We then experiment and, if the results are not entirely satisfactory, may try the task using the other hand to see if it is easier or more efficient. This can be observed when encouraging a young child to undertake a task that he or she has not previously attempted.

It is possible to observe colleagues at work and notice that one will consistently write right handed but always use the left hand to reach for an object or to hold a firearm.

Manual Specialization

In an attempt to understand the process by which we decide which hand to use for a task, scientists have defined the concept of *Manual Specialization*:

Manual Specialization is different from handedness on several dimensions (Young et al, 1983).

Manual Specialization means that the dominant hand is selected for its superior skill in the task being undertaken, when compared to the other hand. This may not be the case when handedness is used to select a hand, because it also considers other factors, such as experience and personal preference.

Manual Specialization is most easily identified on novel, unpracticed, and relatively complex tasks. Handedness tends to evolve after considerable practice on familiar, relatively simple tasks.

Manual Specialization is readily manifested in bimanual co-ordination. Handedness is most often reflected in unilateral activity such as writing.

Because *Manual Specialization* is based solely on skill relevant to the selected task, it may result in either hand being selected to undertake the task as children perform some tasks better with the right hand and others better with the left hand. Handedness usually results in the same preferred hand being selected to undertake a series of tasks.

The tests and exercises set out later in this book have been carefully designed so as to be novel, unpracticed, and sufficiently complex tasks as to test the child's skill whilst being within their ability.

In view of their differing roles it is not surprising that the hands differ in size and strength. Research has shown that in adult men, the dominant right hand is on average 0.25 inch/0.64cm larger in circumference than the left hand but that in adult women the difference is less at about 0.12 inch/ 0.32cm (Young et al, 1983). It is presumed that this greater size is due to greater musculature that would grow out of greater use, and be responsible for the superior development of one side that is reported. Other research has revealed that infants squeeze harder and longer with their right hand than the left hand. (Petrie and Peters, 1980). It has been shown that the difference between the two hands will not be apparent until the 14th or 15th year.

Handedness of brain lateralization

If asked how many brains that you had, most of us would quickly respond with the answer one. We have all seen some medical or crime scene drama program on television in which a brain is removed from some hapless victim. Recently, however, researchers are debating whether we have one brain with a right hemisphere and a left hemisphere or actually that we may have two brains, linked in serial or in parallel, and working together. They also debate whether the "two brains" if that is what they are, are exactly identical or whether there are differences between them. It is a very interesting proposition. Until proved otherwise, this text will presume that we have just one brain, divided into two hemispheres.

We certainly know, however, that each hemisphere, whether it be a separate brain or a half of the whole brain, is used for different purposes. For example, the left hemisphere specializes in language, mathematics, and logical activities whereas the right hemisphere is dominant in visual imagery, music, face recognition, and spatial abilities. We also know that, in general, the right hemisphere controls the left hand side of the body and that the left hemisphere controls the right side of our body. Handedness has its root in our brain.

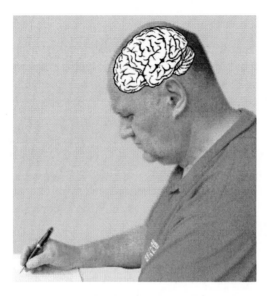

Figure 2-1- Different hemispheres control opposite side of the body.

Sensory information from the left side of the body crosses over to the right side of the brain and information from the right side of the body crosses over to the left side of the brain (Price, 2009). However, the two hemispheres are dominant for different special abilities, but they work together and share information through millions of nerve fibers that are located between the two hemispheres. Scientists believe that the ability of the brain hemispheres to manage different tasks increases the brain's efficiency. Psychologists at the University of Auckland in New Zealand, point out that, "There is an advantage to cerebral dominance because it localizes function to one hemisphere, otherwise, information has to cross back and forth across the two brain binding section, and that can sometimes cause problems." (Corballis et al. 2008).

If 64% of the people on this planet are strongly right-handed and only 11% are left-handed and 25% are mixed handed with no strong hand preference and therefore no dominant hand then most people will have a lateralized or asymmetrical brain. This is an important issue for mental health. Less-lateralized brains may also be linked to lower IQ scores. One study found that left-handers and right-handers had similar IQ scores, but people who identify as ambidextrous had slightly lower scores, especially in arithmetic, memory, and reasoning.

Why do we need a lateralized brain?

What would happen if we had two symmetrical hemispheres in the brain and both sides did the same work and simply shared it out between them? The work would not be done as well or as quickly as it is with a lateralized brain, in which the individual specialisms of the hemispheres enable us to cope more successfully with changing environmental demands (Rogers, 2000).

In fact, this characteristic of the human brain permits a wider range of functions to be carried out effectively than if both sides processed information in exactly the same way. This feature does however have limitations when one region of the lateralized brain is damaged and its ability to control specific tasks are lost and cannot be recovered as fully by other regions. For this reason the ability of different regions of the brain to co-operate in order to perform the specialisms of other, injured, parts of the brain is higher in a non-lateralized brain.

In human development there are critical periods. There are periods when nothing appears to be happening and then there may be a developmental spurt when several things happen at once. In fact, the onset and duration of maturation in different body systems such as neural, muscular, and skeletal is different. A great deal of scientific evidence confirms that the brain is particularly sponge like during the first few years of life, enabling children to absorb new skills quickly and easily. One part of brain development may depend on opportunities to sense and perceive environment, whilst another part is related to a learning process.

Hemisphere lateralization begins at birth. Most newborn children prefer to use the right side of their body to control their head position, their reflex reactions and involuntary movement in response to stimulus (Grattan et al, 1992; Ronnqvist & Hopkins, 1998). Some brain studies have revealed the greater brain activity in the left hemisphere while listening to speech sounds. In contrast, the right hemisphere reacted more to other, non-speech sounds. In addition, children showed a similar brain activity to adolescents and adults while performing motor and cognitive tasks. Apparently, huge processing of acquiring motor, cognitive, and language skills promotes brain lateralization (Berk, 2008).

Development of handedness

As previously discussed, handedness is an ability that is strongly related to brain lateralization. Handedness reflects the ability of one side of the brain to carry out skilled movements and by the age of 6 months, infants display a more efficient reaching movement with their right arm (Hinojosa et al, 2003; Ronnqvist & Domellof, 2006). Generally, handedness extends to the simple, routine skills such as eating, throwing, catching, drawing, and writing (Berk, 2008).

The human brain exercises the same preferences for language that it does for movement. A person with a left side dominance for movement that is reflected in a dominant right hand, will also use the left side of the brain for language. A person with a right side dominance for movement that is reflected in a dominant left hand, will use the right side of the brain for language. This means that 64% of the population use the left side of their brain to deal with language, 11% of the population use the right side of their brain to deal with language and 25% have no strong preference and in some way share language between the hemispheres. This is another indicator of a less lateralized brain (Szaflaraski et al., 2002).

Some developmental studies have shown that the onset of bimanual handedness is related to speech development. They reported that both skills start to develop by the age of 12 months and that this might reflect a dependence upon the presence of hemisphere specialization (Ramsay, 1980). Some ultrasound studies suggest that the formation of handedness actually takes place before birth with many children expressing a preference for their right hand by sucking their right thumb in the fetus by the tenth week of gestation.

Despite agreement on the development of the areas controlling speech and handedness, the association between them is very low with left handed adults (70%) having left hemisphere control of language and right handed adults (96%). This low relationship clearly shows that other factors impact on the relationship. Some scientists argue that the lateralization of hemisphere is multidimensional and includes other aspects of brain function such as visual perception, spatial mapping, and the processing of emotion. These functions have been linked to right hemisphere activity in adults and this dependency is not necessarily reliant on left hemisphere language processing (Young et al, 1983).

One study found that there is no dependency between hemisphere dominance for language and spatial skills (Bryden, et al, 1982). Thus, language is not the only function of brain lateralization and the brain has multiple functions to be considered for lateralization and for explaining handedness. In addition, it is considered that hand function is not a single construct. In fact, the two hands may specialize for different functions even in early infancy, suggesting that different forms of hand preference exist.

Reaching and grasping are manual tasks that children start between 3-4 months of age and which require a hand preference. Research evidence reports that reaching in early infancy is a left-hand preference (Gesell and Ames, 1947), although other researchers report a similar trend for infants aged between 1-4 months. Later, the left-hand preference shifts to a right-hand preference when the child reaches 4.5 months old.

In contrast, there are other studies that reveal a right-hand preference for reaching and exploring activities in the early infancy (Ferre et al, 2010). Grasping is also reported as a right-hand activity. When an object is placed in one hand or another, the grasp is both stronger and longer in duration with the right hand. Overall, it is concluded that the left hand is preferred when there is clearly non-directional activity such as reflexive arm movement or passive holding (Nalcaci et al, 2001). Alternatively, the right hand is preferred for directional, target-related activity such as precision grasping and reaching. This is true regardless of the distance of the target from the hand.

Some manual tasks are performed by two hands in a bimanual movement, for example opening the lid of a container where one hand holds the container and the other hand opens it. Infants use two hands for manipulating objects in different ways in which the signs of brain lateralization and handedness are clearly observable. For example, in an infant 11 months old, it can be observed that the right hand is used for manipulating an object while the left hand holds it and support it (Ramsay, 1980).

Similar findings are also reported for infants below 11 months old as well as for adults. These results suggest that the right hand is more linked to the goal of the movement (access to a target in space). It is proposed that this co-operation between the two hands is more likely to shift attention to the right hand than to the left hand because of the active role of the right hand in the execution of the action and the limitation in attention capacity.

How does lateralization apply to such situations?

When both hands are involved in beginning an action simultaneously, motor commands are first transmitted to the right hemisphere and then, after a delay, to the left hemisphere. In this way a single programmer can initiate movement in the two hands at the same time, but the movement can be controlled and co-ordinated by both hemispheres working in conjunction.

In an interesting study on the development of handedness, seven infants were assessed from the ages of 2 to 10 years and the study concluded that the instability of infant handedness indicated that the hand preference of infants could not be used as an indicator or predictor of adult handedness Other research has revealed that handedness does not consolidate into a stable and robust condition until about 8-11 years of age (Gesell & Ames, 1947).

Children as young as 3 years show an adult-like bias to their right side in the distribution of their handedness (Annett, 1970). Children younger than 8-9 years would readily use their non-preferred hand if the task challenged the using of their preferred hand due to some situational condition such as an obstacle (Connolly & Elliot, 1972. Older children and adults continue to use their preferred hand in such conditions. The influence of situational conditions, socio-cultural pressure, training, and the acquisition of specific manual skills are more likely to have a greater effect on individual handedness before it has consolidated at 8-11 years of age (Coren et al, 1981).

Why is the development of handedness unstable?

It is very hard to answer this question simply because the complexity of handedness means that a number of different factors contribute to hand our hand use preference during the course of our development into full adulthood.

Based on the scientific evidence there are two important theories about the instability of handedness. One of them describes a maturational model based on head-orientation preference, proposed by Gesell and Ames (1947) and the second one describes a multi- factor model and is proposed by Annett (1978).

The first theory proposes that the neonatal supine head-orientation preference is significantly predictive of infant hand use preferences during infancy, especially until the first 14 months. However, the baby's postnatal head orientation is a somewhat better predictor of consistent hand use preference, so that infants with a preference for orienting their heads to the right prefer to use their right hand for reaching, whereas infants who prefer to orient their heads to the left prefer to use their left hand.

It seems that the head orientation preference results in the dominant hand coordinating its movements with the eye on the same side of the body as well as the neural functions of the hand muscles. Since visual information is important to control of hand actions thus development of certain sensory and motor co-ordination will be dominant in later daily life.

The second theory argues that there is an asymmetry in neural and motor commands that is inherited from the parents and which can be clearly seen at birth due to the predominant effect of neural factors rather than environment on the development of behaviors. This asymmetry is perpetuated by other factors such as visualization of the right hand or left hand and reflex reactions.

This suggests that due to different maturation pace in different systems, each system can be lateralized independently. In addition, lateralization of different systems is affected by certain environmental factors such as cultural pressure and vulnerability of the left hemisphere to hypoxia (oxygen deficiency) around the time of birth. In summary, the factors determining handedness may be different at different times and one of the important factors is to identify points of transition between lateral preferences (Young et al, 1983).

Origins of handedness

Some scientists believe that the origin of handedness is genetic. One genetic theory proposes that most children inherit a gene that gives them a bias for right-handedness and a left-dominant brain hemisphere, but that this bias is not strong enough to overcome environmental pressures that might sway children toward a preference for their left-hand.

Family study has not confirmed this genetics theory. For example, Perelle and Ehrman (1994) in a study of over 12,000 subjects reported that 76% of right-handed and 61% of left-handed subjects had no left-handed first-degree relatives. One study that reviewed over thirty five pieces of research that have been conducted on twins suggested that the genetics role for handedness is 25% and 75% of handedness is determined by environment. Similar results have been reported from studies of twins in other countries such as the Netherlands, Finland, and Australia (Vouksimaa et al, 2009).

Some scientific evidence indicates that maturation of the right and left hemisphere is not synchronized. For example, it shows that several language and movement areas of the brain developed 1 to 2 weeks earlier on the right side than on the left side.

According to the above-mentioned studies if the environment has a significant role in determining handedness then habits and practice could facilitate the formation of handedness in infancy and early childhood. The influence of such environmental factors due to cultural and familial pressures or the demands of the task (e.g. sport settings) is an indicator of the flexibility of the human brain to recruit a hand for different purposes (De Agostini et al, 1997). One scientific study reported that body position could affect handedness or cause infants to spend more time looking at and using one hand, which may contribute to greater skill development.

According to Annett's genetic model (1972), most people inherit a disposition to be right-handed, whereas others inherit no disposition at all. Whether hand preference is weaker or simply more variable in infants with familial sinistrality, is unclear. If they are, we might expect the hand preference of such infants to be more sensitive to environmental influences. The effect of practice on the hand preference was not overlooked in the previous scientific literature. For instance, in Taiwan the use of the left hand for writing and eating is deliberately proscribed, only 0.7% of elementary school and college students use the left hand compared with 6.5% of Oriental school children in the United States. This difference is a reflection of the extent to which natural left-hand preference can be suppressed under certain circumstances.

Experiencing and practicing new movement skills might link to hand preferences in the early years of life. Some researchers reported that when infants practice postural and locomotor skills such as sitting, standing, crawling, and walking the hand preference is changed during reaching for an object (Berger et al, 2011). It seems that the instability of hand use during infancy might be related to the onset of new skills and the brain reorganizes the movement planning so that the co-operation between different systems is enhanced (Corbetta et al, 2006).

Handedness is related to the execution of different movement skills (Nalcaci et al, 2001). In some cases the complexity of movement could determine the hand preference. For example, handedness is stronger for complex motor skills requiring extensive training such as eating with utensils, writing, and executing sport skills. We can execute simpler tasks with both hands without any difference in the form and consequence of performance. It is very easy to carry a bag with one hand and then switch the bag and carry it with the opposite hand without any deterioration in performance.

The proportion of left-handers can vary from 1% (Hecaen & Ajuriaguerra, 1964) to 40% (Starosta, 2004) and from one country to another (Perelle & Ehrman, 1994). It is estimated that there are about 240 million left-handed people around the world. Several facts have supported some influence of cultural factors on left-handedness frequency. Cultural conditions can enhance or reduce the magnitude of the hand use preference. Even early in infancy subtle socio-cultural conditions can favor right-hand use. There is undoubtedly societal pressure in favor of right-hand preference (Payne, 1987). This is exerted by handling practices during infancy, parental modeling of manual behaviors, provision of tools suited to right-hand use, and social disapproval of left handedness.

In some cultures it is reported that the cultural pressure prohibits the left hand use for food-related activities. This is the case in Muslim countries, as well as in many Asian countries. In these countries, the left hand is often considered to be impure and is not to be used for feeding. In such situations the frequency of left-handers falls to around 5% or even lower. In Tanzania, East Africa, where children are physically restrained and punished for favoring the left hand, less than 1 % of adults are left-handed (Provins, 1997).

In China, where left handedness is strongly discouraged, activities such as eating and writing are performed with the right hand by persons who otherwise prefer left hand for less-socialized activities. Without any evidence to confirm the influence of culture on changing the proportion of right hander and left hander, therefore socio-cultural pressures are unlikely sources for the initial occurrence and universal distribution of the human handedness.

Males outperform females at hand speed and this is generally accepted as being due to males having a basic motor-speed advantage due to having more muscle fibers. Females have more asymmetry than males in right-left hand speed difference and therefore display a stronger preference for their dominant hand in speed tasks. Also, right handed females tend to have a more asymmetrical motor function. Neuropsychological studies support this view and point out that such differences are due to the structural differences of the brain between the two genders (Young et al., 1983).

Figure 2-2- Environment constrains hand use during child development.

Motor asymmetry in females might explain their better verbal motor function and their greater bi-hemispheric control. Hemispheric specialization has advantages but comes at a price. Right-handed females tend to have a faster right hand than left hand and better fluency in speech, but have less bimanual co-ordination due to less inter-hemispheric communication between the specialized areas of the brain in the execution of movement. In contrast, right-handed males have better bimanual co-ordination but less fluency in speech.

Despite brain lateralization assisting to develop the skills necessary to use the two hands independently, it is reported that some people can use both hands successfully in order to execute a task. Of course this concept is different from bimanual dexterity that is described earlier in this chapter. The terms of adaptability and adjustment are applicable in handedness when right-handers and left-handers adjust to the situation that is prepared for the opposite hander. In fact, due to some cultural pressure mentioned earlier it is possible that the left-handers tried to quickly adjust to their environment. In sport there are some cases that show how the situation of practice led to strengthening the non-dominant hand so that its performance is similar to the dominant hand.

A well- known example of a person being able to use both hands equally well is Kimiko Date Krumm, a naturally left-handed tennis player from Japan, whose family put her under pressure to use her right hand whilst playing. Date Krumm generally holds the racquet in her right hand when playing but transfers it to her forbidden left hand for the most critical situations of a game.

Despite the restrictions imposed on her she has succeeded in becoming one of the leading tennis players in the world.

Karoly Takacs, a soldier from Hungary, hoped to win an Olympic gold medal in the Pistol Shooting at the Berlin Olympics in 1936, but because he was a sergeant and the competition was restricted to officers, he missed out. In 1938 he lost his right hand due to an accident with a faulty grenade and in 1940 and 1944 the Olympic Games were cancelled due to the Second World War. He eventually overcame his bad luck to win two Olympic gold medals, in London in 1948 and in Helsinki in 1952, holding his pistol in his left-hand (Jokl, 1981).

Andrzej Grubba, a World Championship bronze medalist in table tennis, was a naturally left-handed player but scored his greatest successes in the international arena while playing with his right hand. Grubba became famous for his ability to change playing hands mid-rally. He was not forced to make the change away from using his dominant left hand, but rather he discovered the value of swapping hands mid match in order to confuse his opponents.

M. Strupler, a left-handed handball player, played for a team in the First Division of the Swiss League for 15 years. Feeling the need to fit in with his right handed team mates, he worked on perfecting all the techniques of the game using both hands. In this way he had an advantage over other players as an ambidextrous player is a much more confusing and dangerous opponent to face. Eventually, his left-handed throws were not as successful as his right handed ones and his coach threatened to substitute him if he continued using his left hand to take throws (Stadler & Bucher, 1986).

Summary

We use different hands to undertake different tasks. Handedness is most often reflected in unilateral activity such as writing. The human brain is created asymmetrical so that it controls all aspects of the two hands independently. The two hands differ structurally and functionally in terms of their weight, size, and strength.

Brain lateralization means the right side of the brain controls the left hand and the left side of the brain control right hand. Most people have a lateralized or asymmetrical brain and a few people have not and are mixed handed. Hemisphere lateralization begins at birth but it is not stable during human development and does not settle until 10 year of age. Scientific evidence indicates that the maturation of the right and left hemisphere is not synchronized and this might lead to hand use preference.

The influence of situational conditions, socio-cultural pressure, training, and the acquisition of specific manual skills are more likely greater on individual handedness status before handedness has consolidated. There are two important ideas about the instability of handedness: the maturational model and the multifactor model.

Scholars believe that genetics and environment are two important determinants for hand use preference. The scientific studies suggested that the genetics role for handedness is 25% and 75% of handedness is determined by environment. Experiencing and practicing new movement skills might link to hand preferences in the early years of life. Handedness is stronger for complex motor skills that require extensive training whereas it is possible that in simple movement tasks we use both hands with equal ability.

Cultural conditions can enhance or reduce the magnitude of the hand use preference. In some cultures it is reported that the cultural pressure prohibits the left hand use for writing and food-related activities. Females have more asymmetry than males in right-left hand speed difference. In spite of brain lateralization for using hands independently it is reported that some people could use both hands successfully in executing different tasks especially sport skills.

Chapter 3

CHILDREN WHO ARE MIXED HANDED (INCLUDING AMBIDEXTROUS OR AMBIVALENT)

Introduction

About 25% of the population are mixed handed. Mixed handed people have no dominant hand and a symmetrical brain that is unlike that of other people, who possess a strong right or strong left handed preference. Research has linked the non-lateralized brain with lower Intelligence Quotient (I.Q.) scores.

Evidence from a large-scale study of 11-year olds in the United Kingdom suggests that mixed handed individuals may be disadvantaged in tests of verbal reasoning, non-verbal reasoning, reading, and mathematical skills when compared to those with a strong right or strong left-hand preference. The results were not, however, replicated in another study of boys in Germany although these boys were younger than those in the U.K. survey.

Research conducted in conjunction with a television show in which members of the public were given an IQ test, asked individuals to state whether they wrote with their right hand, left hand, or with either-hand. The results supported the earlier finding that mixed handed individuals perform less well than left or right handers, especially on sub-scales measuring arithmetic skills, memory, and reasoning, and extended that finding to adults (Corballis et al, 2008).

Many famous people have been mixed handed. Michelangelo (1475-1564) was a multi-faceted genius like Leonardo da Vinci. He often painted with both hands, so that when one got tired, he switched to the other. The British artist, Sir Edwin Henry Landseer (1802-1873) could draw with both hands simultaneously. He taught drawing and etching to Queen Victoria (1819-1901) who was a lefty who later became mixed handed.

Sir Alexander Fleming (1881-1955) (who discovered penicillin), Albert Einstein (1879-1955) (author of the Theory of Relativity), and Nikola Tesla (1856-1943) (who promoted the use of electricity by advocating the advantages of alternating current) were all mixed handed. Benjamin Franklin (1706-1790) (polymath and Founding Father of the U.S.A.) was also mixed handed and signed the Declaration of Independence and the Constitution with his left hand.

In this chapter the problems surrounding mixed handedness will be discussed and related to recent research. The scope of the discussion will be around the concept of mixed handedness, mixed handedness in non-human species, comparison between mixed handedness and ambidexterity, the causes of mixed handedness, the impact of mixed handedness on human abilities, and other kinds of symmetry in the body.

Concept and definition of Mixed Handed People

These are people who display no strong preference for either their right or left hand, who may use either hand to undertake a specific task, who may use different hands to undertake different tasks or who swap hands more than occasionally when undertaking a task. The group includes those who are ambidextrous and those who are ambivalent.

In fact, it is quite advantageous in certain sports and martial arts to be able to use both hands with equal facility. The Greeks encouraged and tried to promote mixed handedness because it was simply logical in both sports and battle to be adept with both hands instead of just one. The advantage of surprise, derived from using the left hand, is explained in the Bible:

"And Ehud put forth his left hand, and took the dagger from his right thigh,.. being, as before observed, a left handed man, and this he could the better do, without being taken notice of by the king, who, if he saw him move his left hand, would have no suspicion of his going to draw a dagger with it" (Judges 3:15-16).

Mixed handedness may be considered to be in opposition to the usual hand preference as it does not require a lateralized brain. If we have the same skilled hands to perform the usual tasks of daily life we will have an advantage because of our improved adaptability. If ambidexterity makes people more able to adapt to their environment, then what is the purpose of handedness? What advantage does it provide? (Bishop, 1990).

At first glance it would appear logical for us to use both hands equally and interchangeably, but if you compared the human brain with a computer, this computer would require considerably enhanced levels of memory and processing power in order to achieve this. In practice, the only way in which we can achieve such precision and speed of movement with the current capacities of the human brain is to employ the principles of brain laterality with its recognized specialisms and to identify a dominant hand for each task. Currently, this system seems to work for 90% of the adult population.

Provins et al (1987) asked students to rate seventy five activities in their daily lives on a seven point scale to indicate whether they preferred to use their right hand, their left hand or whether they had no hand preference when undertaking the task. Their results revealed that in writing more than 98% of people always preferred to use their dominant hand. Similar results were revealed in other activities such as playing with a tennis racquet, throwing a dart, pulling a trigger on a gun, painting and drawing, and for other precision activities.

In other tasks, where high level skills were not required, but where muscle exhaustion may have been a factor, such as carrying a suitcase, grasping an object in a power grip, and holding dog lead, they did not express any hand preference. These results indicate that where skill is important in their daily activities people prefer to use their dominant hand rather than to select a hand at random.

As previously discussed, the lateralized brain has functional advantages in that it localizes each task to one hemisphere as a specialism, thus avoiding information passing back and forth across the binding situated between the two hemispheres, which can sometimes cause problems (Corballis et al, 2008). In fact, our bodies perform more efficiently when our motor control systems specialize so that each hand performs a different role rather than for both hands to learn to perform a variety of roles.

There are, however, many situations in our daily lives in which we must undertake bimanual tasks, such as, for example, where you are reading this book and one hand is holding the book and the other hand is used to turn over the pages, so that the two hands perform complementary tasks. Frequently, the ultimate success in performance in such tasks will depend on the co-ordination between the hands.

What is the logic behind lateralized brain and handedness? We can explain the values of handedness into two logics: learning of a skill and interference problem (Bishop, 1990).

The learning of a movement skill is a multi-stage process during which the learner needs to pass through certain stages in a specific period of time in order to master the skill (Schmidt & Wrisberg, 2004). In the early stages of the process, the performance is very slow and poorly co-ordinated and relies on feedback for corrective adjustment of the movement.

Acquisition of the skill requires practice and repetition, so that after extensive practice the movement is executed in a well co-ordinated fashion, with less conscious effort, but more quickly and with fewer errors. At this stage the learner does not rely on feedback to correct the movement as it can be executed as a pre-programmed and skillful action.

As a skill is learned, the precision of the movement is refined so that the action of each bone, joint and muscle is co-ordinated so as to improve efficiency, increase co-operation and reduce interference. In this way handedness will become most apparent in highly skilled movements that require practice in order to achieve mastery. Of course, the nature of the skill is also important, so that hand use preference is required more in precision skills than in other type of activity (Provins et al, 1987).

One problem with using the two hands interchangeably is due to the interference phenomena. This is where we learn a skills with one hand and then swap hands and attempt the task with the other hand. Our learning is interrupted and skills may be lost. If we then swap hands again, back to the original hand, our learning is interrupted again and the skills may be lost again. For example, when writing it is an advantage to restrict learning to one hand because if we attempt to switch between the two hands there could be interference between the different parts of the movements learned by each hand, rather than any actual positive transfer of learning.

Pictures 3-1- Some daily activities require cooperation between two hands.

In our repertoire of motor skills we have the ability to perform certain tasks as a form of mirror-image (by reversing the direction of movement from the right to the left or vice versa), but for writing it would not be effective (Lazarus & Todor, 1987). For example, writing your home address in the usual left to right direction would allow it to be generally read but reversing the direction of the script would produce something that almost nobody could understand.

In contrast, interference in brushing the teeth would mean using the left hand to move the brush from the left to the right side of the mouth, and then switching the brush to the right hand and using the right hand to move from left to right and vice versa, which would not be a problem. In fact, some tasks cannot be performed with either hand and some tools cannot be used with both hands. These include screwdrivers, corkscrews and can openers that only work in one direction.

Ambidexterity in non-human species

Research has revealed that unlike humans many non-human species are mixed handed. Warren (1980) found paw preference in individual animals such as cats, rats and monkeys, but the distribution of preferences is quite different from that in humans and the animals showed a high proportion of inconsistent preference. Thus, hand preference is a unique phenomenon in humans and this argues against the view that handedness is due to evolution.

Other scholars (MacNeilage et al, 1987; Lehman, 1987) have argued that the in Old World monkeys there was evidence of consistent hand preference which is overlooked because of the form of dominant hand use. In fact, they stated that while animals try to show a left hand preference for reaching for food, they show a right hand preference for manipulative skills. It appears that animals use both hands for different purposes and that this could not be an indicator of ambidexterity in non-human species.

Animals like humans displayed hand preference according to the nature of the task being undertaken. As previously discussed, hand preference should be apparent in highly skilled activities in humans. If arguments against the Warren study are correct then we should expect to see consistent handedness in animals in such activities and in bimanual co-ordination tasks.

Chimpanzees fishing for termites are a popular example of a highly skilled activity in animals. The chimpanzees show considerable proficiency in probing termite nests with stalks and developing a precision grip through extensive practice over a period of years. This skill is a type of activity that requires precision of movement and practice to execute skillfully. Research shows that the chimpanzees are absolutely ambidextrous in this activity (Goodall, 1986). The same research also reported on some other highly skilled activities by chimpanzees, such as cracking open fruit, which showed a consistent hand preference.

Further research studied three language-trained chimpanzees with an inventory of skills. It revealed a lack of hand preference in gross motor ballistic tasks, but revealed a hand preference in fine motor sequential tasks (Bolser et al, 1988). Other research reported an equal number of right-handers and left-handers in a group of 10 captive lowland gorillas involved in a reaching for food task (Fagot and Vauclair, 1988).

Observation of four captive lowland gorillas picking up apple wedges revealed that in 96 % of occasions they displayed a right hand preference (Fischer et al, 1982). However, other research found that wild mountain gorillas when picking up pieces of food showed no hand preference and would reach out with whichever hand was nearest to the food (Schaller, 1963) Many scientists working in animal research believe that task selection is important in assessing animal handedness.

It appears that it is not possible to extract any firm conclusion about animal handedness from the available research. The variability of the techniques and methods applied to the observation of the animal behaviors during different tasks has resulted in a considerable variability within and between species that require further investigation before any conclusions can be reached. Therefore, Warren's opinion that handedness is a unique feature only observable in humans is not supported by other scientific studies.

Mixed Handedness and Ambidexterity

It is important that handedness is studied across a range of different people. The testing of handedness will be discussed in more detail in chapters 5 and 6 but understanding the assessment system is important in terms of distinguishing between mixed handedness and ambidexterity. Are there any differences between mixed handedness and ambidexterity? Or are they synonymous terms that may be used interchangeably?

Before answering this question we need to answer another crucial question: Should handedness be assessed based on the number of people expressing a preference for their right hand and the number of people expressing a preference for their left hand, or on the basis of numerical data such as a score in the range of 0 to 100 based on the strength of their preference for their right hand or left hand in a range of daily activities?

One advocate for the first proposal believes that handedness should be assessed on the basis of a categorical system (McManus, 1984). He believes that handwriting, as the most strongly lateralized activity, should not be the basis of any strong hand preference (e.g. strong right hand, equal preference in both hands, strong left hand).

The direction of hand preference is influenced by genetic factors that are related to brain lateralization, but a strong hand preference is not controlled by genetics. Handwriting is extremely stable and nobody shows equal proficiency in both hands. Another researcher has supported the continuous assessment system and argues that viewing handedness as a category might be like height in terms of "tall" and "short", but without defining the terms.

One researcher has argued in favor of testing "hand proficiency" rather than "hand preference" as a measure of handedness, and for a continuous testing system capable of assessing the degree of variance in hand proficiency. The task selected for the research requires participants to move ten dowel pegs from one row of holes to another row (Annett, 1970). By assessing the speed at which the participants are able to move the pegs with each of their hands in two separate trials, the test assesses their relative hand proficiency and therefore, their handedness.

What sort of information does the proficiency measurement give us?

Figure 3-2- Hand preference or hand proficiency: the dilemma between ambidexterity and mixed handedness.

The test assesses the proficiency of each hand at performing different skills and places it in a continuum from weak to strong. According to this measurement system, hand proficiency varies from skill to skill, so that one person may have a right hand that is strong at one skill, a left hand that is strong at another skill and they may both be roughly the same at another skill.

One study reported finding that between 25-30 % of children were mixed-handed (Annett, 1972). Another study reported on a group that were left handed for writing, eating with a spoon and combing their hair, but right handed for holding a toothbrush, playing with a tennis racquet, and using scissors (Bishop, 1990). A scientist reviewing these research projects wrote, "Ambilaterality is relatively rare, what this showed is not ambilateraltiy but mixed handedness". True ambilaterality is indeed rare but mixed handedness occurs in some 30% of the population, so that claims to equal skill with both hands must be treated with caution (Porac and Coren, 1981).

A study focusing on six activities including writing, throwing a ball, using a racquet, striking a match, swinging a hammer, and using a toothbrush, reported that 64.7% of males and 61.4% of females were right-handed for all activities, that 2.6% of males and 3.6% of females were left-handed for all activities and that 32.7% of males and 35.0% females were mixed-handed, so that they performed some tasks with their right hand and others with left hand. For example, 4.1% of males and 4.4% of females were right-handed in writing but left-handed for other tasks.

Interestingly, 2.4% males and 3.0% females were left-handed in writing and right-handed for other activities. Overall, the researchers established eight classes of handedness based on the skill sets of the participants and on hand proficiency rather than hand preference. The research also showed that there are subgroups for mixed handedness that are larger than the total number of left-handers (Annett and Kilshaw, 1983).

These studies show that ambidexterity, meaning equal skill with either hand especially for writing, is rare, with an incidence of approximately about 0.3%, but mixed handedness, where changes of handedness between tasks is common, there is an incidence of 30%. One leading researcher has expressed the opinion that cultural and physical (related to the design of tools for right-handed rather than left handed people) pressures have obscured the importance of mixed handedness (Annett, 2002). In fact, these pressure have probably also concealed the true incidence of mixed handedness.

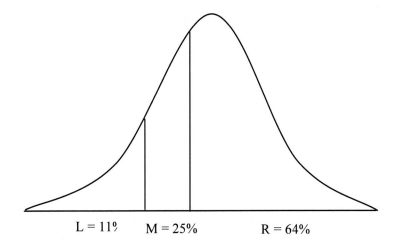

L = 11%   M = 25%   R = 64%

Figure 3-1- Incidences of left handedness (L), mixed handedness (M), and right handedness (R) represented under normal curve (%).

Hand proficiency scores have been found to follow the normal frequency distribution rules in mathematics and are therefore capable of being represented on a normal frequency distribution curve such as the one in Figure

3-1. If the height of the population was plotted on a graph, a curve of the same shape would be generated. If the weight of the population was plotted on a graph, a curve of the same shape would be generated.

The frequency of people who have an average (mean) score is greater than those with the minimum and maximum scores. For example, more than 68% of the population are of average height, whereas 16% are short and 16% are tall. The normal frequency distribution curve can be used as an indicator of distributions of population for features such as handedness. For our purpose, the distribution of different hand proficiency is very similar to normal curve (see figure 3-1).

Causes of ambidexterity or mixed handedness

It has been proposed that mixed handedness might be due to the joint expression of two alleles, one for left and one for right handedness. According to this model, the left gene is not fully recessive but sometimes expressed in heterozygotes (combination of right and left genotypes). In simple terms, there are three genetic classes for handedness: right hand, mixed hand, and left hand. If the frequency of right allele was 0.8, the left allele was 0.2, and then a random pairing would be akin to putting 100 tokens, 80 marked "right" and 20 marked "left" into a bag, and drawing out two at random. On average there would be 64 "right-right", 32 "right-left", and 4 "left-left" pairs. If handedness depends on three genotypes then two right-handed parents would have only right-handed children, and two left-handed parents would have only left-handed children. But, one right-handed parent and one left-handed parent would have mixed handed children.

Annett later modified her theory into more complex genetics and explained that individuals probably do not carry a dominant or recessive gene for right or left handedness *per se*. Rather, most of the population inherited a relatively strong genetic component to be "oriented" toward its right side. The term "right shift factors (RS)" is an expression for the majority of people to have various degrees of bias to dextrality (right hand preference). Thus, most people have this factor (RS +) and a few people (18%) do not (RS -). The distribution of the RS factor in the population is the same as the normal frequency distribution.

The lack of RS factor leads some individuals to be non-right hander (Iaccino, 1993). Thus, according to this revised model, the probability for incidence of RS++ (both parents) in the population is 32%, for RS+- is 50%, and for RS- - is 18%. This means that most children tend to shift from the left to right hand during the development process, but having pure right hand is not a strong genetic trait. It is necessary to mention that children with the RS++ and RS- - are homozygote because they have inherited same alleles from both parents, but children with RS+- are heterozygote because they have inherited different alleles from their parents.

Some scientific studies have proposed that prenatal stress is a factor in the incidence of mixed handedness (Obel et al, 2003). One theory is that the effect of hormonal treatment for infertility as well as the stress associated with it determines handedness. One study investigated the incidence of mixed handedness in children whose mothers were treated for infertility in Denmark (Zhu et al, 2009). It looked at children who were 7 years old and confirmed their mixed handedness in that they used both hands equally. The results showed that the incidence of mixed handedness was higher in children born after infertility treatment; particularly intrauterine insemination (IUI) compared with children of fertile couples.

Children of couples resulting from an unplanned pregnancy were also more likely to be mixed-handed. Such fertilisation methods increase the hormonal-related stress. Another reason for the higher number of mixed handedness in children resulting from intra-uterine insemination (I.U.I.) is the abnormality in the shape of the sperm tail, the organ that is responsible for lateralization (Chodhari et al, 2004). Some studies reported that mixed handedness was strongly associated with parental mixed handedness which is an indicator of a familial factor (Zhu et al, 2009). Other proposed factors such as maternal age, maternal smoking, and the sex of child were also associated with mixed handedness in children.

Hand proficiency impact on different abilities

Having previously distinguished between mixed handedness and ambidexterity, it is now necessary to clarify the association between hand proficiency as a form of mixed handedness with other human abilities in different contexts such as literature, mathematics, art, and sport. The impact of being right handed and left handed and the associated risk of abnormalities will be discussed further in the next chapter.

In order to clarify the effects of different levels of hand proficiency on our ability we should notice the role of heterozygote (RS+-) advantages. A heterozygote profile has the inherited advantage of both sides of the brain, and hence should demonstrate a moderate to skillful degree in most human abilities.

In the 1970s researchers classified school children according to their hand proficiency using a peg moving test and then tested their vocabulary and memory using the Peabody Picture Vocabulary Test and Raven's Cultured Progressive Matrices. The children were classified into four Hand Proficiency groups according to whether they were strong right-handers, moderate right-handers, mild right-handers or left-handers.

The results showed that in both sexes the vocabulary IQ and memory score were higher for the mild and moderate right-handed children. In contrast, both left-handed and strong right-handed had the lowest scores. In respect of educational advantage, the scientific findings revealed that those children with strong hand preferences were less likely to succeed (Annett, 1970b).

Spatial ability tests also showed that neither pure left-handers nor right-handers performed well but that mixed-handers in both sides (right or left-handed) showed better scores.

Researchers submitted a group of students to an applied mathematics test and then classified them according to their hand proficiency score. The results showed that the arithmetic scores were higher in the left-handed students of both sexes. In fact, the frequency of left- writers in the group with superior score in mathematics was 13 %. (Annett and Manning, 1990)

Researchers found that there was an increased incidence of mixed-handedness among instrumentalists when compared with the general population (Byrne, 1974). Other researchers found fewer errors in a test of pitch identification among mixed-handers when compared to strongly right-handers and left-handers (Deutsch, 1980).

In sport, researchers investigated the handedness among groups of athletes competing at different levels of sport. Their results showed that greater ability in sport is related to mixed-handedness. (Porac and Coren, 1981).

Other kinds of symmetry in the body

In the body there are more than two asymmetries according to the different sensory or motor organs. In fact, brain laterality imposes a requirement on other organs to be asymmetrical in their functions. For this reason, we have other organ preferences such as eye dominance, foot dominance, and ear dominance for our daily living tasks that might or might not related to handedness.

The question is whether we have mixed laterality for all above-mentioned organs and limbs. Ipsilaterality and contralaterality are two different terms that refer to using the limbs of one side of the body or different sides of the body, respectively. For example, using right hand and right foot (ipsilateral) or left hand and right foot (contralateral) for performing different task that need the cooperation of different limbs at a same time. Such situations also are applicable for other organs such as using right eye with right hand or left eye with right hand.

It is reported the distribution of eye dominance is different from handedness in which 23 % of people were superior in left eye, 22 % in right eye, and 55 % dominated in both eyes equally. This distribution is different with handedness because the frequency of mixed handedness was 25%. Annett and Turner (1974) reported that right-handed people used left eye for sighting (36%) whereas in the left-handers the frequency of using left eye was higher and equal to 68%. In respect to foot preference, their results showed that about 83.3% left-handers and 4% right-handed used left foot for kicking. For ear preference, Annett (2002) reported that 70% right-handers and left-handers held the telephone receiver in their preferred hand.

These results clarify two important issues about the body laterality. Firstly, it shows the pattern of body laterality follows contralaterality and ipsilaterality in population but the distribution of ipsilaterality is more than contralaterality. Secondly, the mixed laterality of the body depends on the organ and limbs, so that the ipsilaterality is more common between hand/foot and hand/ear rather than in hand/eye.

Summary

About 25% of people are mixed handed. Mixed handed people have no dominant hand and a symmetrical brain unlike other people. Ambidexterity is the ability to use both hands with equal ease or facility. Scientific studies indicated that the handedness rather than ambidextrous is more advantageous for people for in their daily life activities. The reason is that the lateralized brain has advantages functionally because it localizes function to one hemisphere, otherwise, that can cause problems.

The hand preference is a unique phenomenon in humans and unlike humans the non-human species are mixed handed. Of course any conclusion about the animals' handedness is not plausible due to variability within and between species and the nature of the task. One confusing matter for ambidexterity is the difference between hand preference and hand proficiency. Some scientists believe that handedness is an absolute characteristic in humans that should be considered based on nominal scales such as strongly right-handed, strongly left-handed and mixed-handed. Others believe it is a relative feature that could be scored from 0 to 100 for each hand depending on the nature of the skill. For this reason, distinguishing ambidexterity from mixed handedness is not easy in any population.

Mixed handedness means changing the preferred hand between different tasks whereas ambidexterity means using both hands equally for all tasks. Annett proposed that mixed handedness might be due to joint expression of two alleles, one for left and one for right handedness. Other scientists have explained that the cause of mixed handedness is the effect of hormonal treatment for infertility as well as stress associated with it. Other proposed factors for mixed handedness in children were maternal age, maternal smoking, and sex of child. For the most of the abilities the pure right-handed people have a disadvantage in comparison for incidences of left-handers or non-right handedness such as mixed handedness. Hand preference is fairly associated with other kind of the body laterality such as foot, ear, and eye.

Chapter 4

THE NEGATIVE ASPECTS OF HANDEDNESS (WHETHER RIGHT, LEFT OR MIXED OR SWITCHING)

Introduction

In the earlier chapters the history of handedness was reviewed, the factors that affect handedness were discussed and, hopefully, the concerns of parents were refocused from children who are left handed to those who are mixed handed.

This chapter will discuss the negative aspects of the three different forms of possible handedness, whether it be right handedness, left handedness or mixed handedness, as well as the negative aspects of switching hands.

What it means to be strongly right handed

When told that a child is strongly right handed, it is possible to assume that the child has the usual asymmetrical brain, where the skills are shared between the right and left hemispheres of the brain according to the specialisms set out in Figure 1-1. The child will rely on the left hemisphere to control his or her dominant right hand and may be expected to reflect those skills in which the left hemisphere specializes:

- Analytical thought;
- Complex rhythm;
- Language;
- Linearity;
- Lists;
- Logic;
- Mathematics;
- Science;
- Sequence;
- Speech;
- Writing.

The child may reasonably be expected to be weaker in those areas in which the right hemisphere specializes:

- Art;
- Attention;
- Creativity;
- Emotion;
- Inspiration;
- Intuition;
- Language;
- Musical aptitude;
- Perception;
- Pitch and intonation;
- Spatial awareness;
- Synthesis Visual concepts.

For clarity, these are comparative views and do not mean that a strongly right handed child will never be able to appreciate music or to understand more than one language. It means that these areas are not their strongest and may require a little additional effort in order to achieve the desired success.

In the light of the words of the Spanish Jesuit philosopher, Baltasar Gracián (b.1601-d. 1658)"Self-knowledge is the beginning of self-improvement."; this information should be considered positively, and seen as a way to improve.

Negative effects of being right handed

Academic success

One interesting study looked at academic achievement and handedness. In the U.K. all children used to be assessed in national examinations at age 12 (for selection to elite grammar schools) and at age 16 (General Certificate of Secondary Education (GCSE). The students were assessed using a peg moving task to identify their hand proficiency and the results showed that the successful students were 18% strongly right-handed, 22% strongly left-handed and 60% mixed-handed. When this is compared with the usual distribution in society, of 64% strong right handers, 11% strong left handers and 25% mixed handers, it can be easily seen that the right handers are severely underrepresented among the successful students. (Annett, 2002).

Mathematics and English language

Research has shown has strong right handedness is associated with poor performance in Mathematics, English and in I.Q. Tests (Annett, 2002). In the previous chapter it was reported that when students were tested on Vocabulary IQ and Raven's Cultured Matrices tests the results showed that strong right-handers had performed poorly in both tests and that mixed-handers scored well. (Annett 1970 and 1978).

Musical Aptitude

Research has shown that a reduced frequency of right handedness is associated with higher musical ability (Deutsch, 1980). In a test of pitch identification, strongly right- handed and strongly left-handed subjects made more errors than mixed-handed subjects (Deutsch, 1980). Another study found right-handers to be worse than left-handers at identifying rhythms when beats were presented to both ears simultaneously (Craig, 1980). It is also reported that right-handers are weaker in tone perception when compared to left-handers (Craig, 1980). In view of all this evidence it cannot be surprising that strongly right-handed people are less frequently successful musicians (Ellis et al., 1988).

Spatial awareness

Spatial awareness is the ability to conceptualize the size, shape, distance, speed and depth of objects in space. It is an essential skill for those driving motor vehicles or playing ball games, who desire to find a way to their goal and avoid all potential obstacles in their path. It is reported that as the strength of the right-handedness increases spatial awareness decreases (Annett, 2002).

Sport

Research has revealed that the frequency of left-handers increases in the athletic population (Porac and Coren, 1981). Research has shown that a third of top class fencers are left handed (Azemar, 1993).

Manual Skills

Researchers classified children into three groups, of strong right-handers, strong left-handers, and mixed-handers, based on the hand that they used for writing and drawing. They then tested the children's manual skills using a peg moving task, using first their preferred hand and then their non-preferred hand. The results showed an association between poor performance and consistent right-hand preference and between poor performance and using the non-preferred hand (Kilshaw and Annett, 1983).

Figure 4-1- Strong-handedness reflects an asymmetrical brain.

What it means to be strongly left handed

When told that a child is strongly left handed, it is possible to assume that the child has the usual asymmetrical brain, where the skills are shared between the right and left hemisphere of the brain according to the specialisms set out in Figure 1-1. The child will rely on the right hemisphere to control his or her dominant left hand and may be expected to reflect those skills in which the right hemisphere specializes:

- Art;
- Attention;
- Creativity;
- Emotion;
- Inspiration;
- Intuition;
- Language;
- Musical aptitude;
- Perception;
- Pitch and intonation;
- Spatial awareness.
- Synthesis Visual concepts.

The child may reasonably be expected to be weaker in those areas in which the right hemisphere specializes:

- Analytical thought;
- Complex rhythm;
- Language;
- Linearity;
- Lists;
- Logic;
- Mathematics;
- Science;
- Sequence;
- Speech;
- Writing.

For clarity, these are comparative views and do not mean that a strongly left handed child will never be able to talk or write clearly. It means that these areas are not their strongest and may require a little additional effort in order to achieve the desired success.

In the light of the words of the Spanish Jesuit philosopher, Baltasar Gracián (b.1601-d. 1658)"Self-knowledge is the beginning of self-improvement."; this information should be considered positively, and seen as a way to improve.

Negative effects of Left Handedness

The incidence of left handedness has been associated with slightly raised levels of a number of other conditions. The reasons for this coincidence is not fully understood, but are believed to include factors including birth stress, hypoxia (lack of oxygen) at and around the time of birth and lesions on the brain.

The risk of a child possessing one of these conditions, whilst raised, are not high and should not cause alarm. The information is included here as it may assist a few families to understand situations in which they may find themselves. These conditions include:

- Autism
- Cerebral palsy
- Dyslexia
- Epilepsy
- Mental retardation
- Schizophrenia

The conditions have been outlined as follows:

Autism

"Autism is a lifelong developmental disability that affects how a person communicates with, and relates to, other people. It also affects how they make sense of the world around them... Autism is very often diagnosed alongside other conditions, such as dyslexia, dyspraxia, attention deficit hyperactivity disorder (ADHD) and learning disabilities." (National Autism Society, 2011). It is a spectrum condition with symptoms ranging from slight to severe, although there are also people with High Performing Autism (H.P.A.). In its early stages it is sometimes confused with Schizophrenia.

Cerebral palsy

"A group of permanent disorders of the development of movement and posture, causing activity limitations that are attributed to non-progressive disturbances that occurred in the developing fetal or infant brain. The motor disorders of cerebral palsy are often accompanied by disturbances of sensation, perception, cognition, communication and behavior, by epilepsy and by secondary musculoskeletal problems." (Rosenbaum et al., 2007).

As the injury or illness causing cerebral palsy occurs at or before birth and the condition is usually identified by the age of two years, and handedness is not established until the age of six years, any issues with cerebral palsy are likely to have been identified by the time that handedness becomes an issue.

Dyslexia

"Dyslexia is a broad term defining a learning disability that impairs a person's fluency or comprehension accuracy in being able to read and which can manifest itself as a difficulty with phonological awareness, phonological decoding, orthographic coding, auditory short-term memory, or rapid naming." (Wikipedia, 2011).

A study undertaken at a clinic in London and at a nearby school looked at hand proficiency and reading quotation. It found that 18.6% of those with Dyslexia were left handed, as compared to 8.2% of the control group. In respect to reading ability, the research showed that left-handers had lower reading scores and identified phonological problem such as the ability to distinguish similar words such as "SUN", "GUN", "FUN" (Annett, 2002).

Epilepsy

"Epilepsy is currently defined as a tendency to have recurrent seizures (sometimes called fits). A seizure is caused by a sudden burst of excess electrical activity in the brain, causing a temporary disruption in the normal message passing between brain cells. This disruption results in the brain's messages becoming halted or mixed up. The brain is responsible for all the functions of your body, so what you experience during a seizure will depend on where in your brain the epileptic activity begins and how widely and rapidly it spreads. For this reason, there are many different types of seizure and each person will experience epilepsy in a way that is unique to them" (Epilepsy Action, 2011).

Although all the factors listed above have been identified with causing epilepsy, in 60% of cases, no cause can be confirmed.

Mental retardation

Although the term, "Mental retardation" is starting to be considered as politically incorrect, it is scientifically accurate and, as yet, no suitable alternative term has yet been accepted into universal use, so it will be used here and amended as and when an alternative is available.

"Mental retardation (MR) is a generalized disorder appearing before adulthood, characterized by significantly impaired cognitive functioning and deficits in two or more adaptive behaviors. It has historically been defined as an Intelligence Quotient score under 70". (Wikipedia, 2011).

Researchers have identified higher rates of familial sinistrality among left-handed mentally retarded people than among other left-handers. "The reasoning behind this notion is that a family history of left-handedness may be mediated by a familial tendency to have birth stress or may be associated with an anomalous intrauterine environment for the developing fetus (Searleman et al., 1988) (p.133). Another study showed the higher prevalence of familial left-handedness in mentally handicapped individuals (Pipe, 1987).

Schizophrenia

"Schizophrenia is a complex illness in which people have difficulties in their thought processes leading to hallucinations, delusions, disordered thinking and unusual speech or behavior (known as 'psychotic symptoms')" (American Psychiatric Association, 2004).

Scientists from the University of Oxford have discovered a gene called "LRRTMI" that affects left-handers and predisposes them to psychotic illnesses like schizophrenia (Franck, 2007). Left-handed individuals usually interchange functions between their two hemispheres and this modifies the symmetry in their brain. The imbalance in the brain facilities psychotic conditions such as schizophrenia that *per se* is an unusual balance in the brain. Impairment of brain symmetry is reported to be linked with schizophrenia and this is more observable in left-handers than right-handers.

Researchers in England and Sweden have reported that the number of left-handers in a group of children with reading and spelling difficulties is twice that in a control group of other children (Annett, 2002).

What it means to be mixed handed

When told that a child is mixed handed, it is possible to assume that the child has a symmetrical brain, unlike some other children, and that tasks are randomly shared between the hemispheres. Each hand will be controlled by the opposite hemisphere of the brain.

Negative effects of mixed handedness

Most children experiment with using both hands for most tasks as infants and researchers have confirmed this by reporting that children between the ages of 18 and 42 months show inconsistent handedness (Gottfried and Bathurst, 1983). There appears to be a general consensus among most researchers that most children do not resolve their handedness issues and decide on their preferences until they reach the age of six years. Clearly, this has the potential to cause difficulties at schools which take children before that age.

A study of 12,770 11 years old children in the U.K. studied the association between mixed handedness and intellectual ability. They found that those children who failed to show a hand preference had lower scores on verbal ability, non-verbal ability, reading comprehension, and mathematical ability that indicated a "hemispheric indecision" effect on intellectual ability (Crow et al., 1998).

A study conducted through New Zealand television asked participants to specify their hand preference for writing before undertaking a battery of tests. It then reported that mixed handed people showed a lower IQ score on six tests involving language, memory, spatial ability, reasoning, arithmetic, and social knowledge. The researchers explained some parts of their findings based on brain lateralization. They postulated that the lack of lateralization that is seen in some conditions such as magical ideation in schizophrenia is responsible for poor intellectual ability in mixed handed people (Corballis et al., 2008).

Another large-scale study that was carried out on the internet showed that verbal fluency was lower in people with no established hand preference for writing (Corballis et al., 2008).

Samuel Orton, a Consultant Neurologist in New York in 1937 and possibly the world's first Human Movement Scientist, noted that many of the children referred to him for developmental language problems were mixed handed (Annett, 2002).

Negative effects of switching

The recent and highly publicized, Oscar-winning film entitled, "The Kings Speech" of 2010, based on the life and times of King George VI, who acceded to the U.K. Throne in 1936, has highlighted the social, emotional and psychiatric problems associated with stuttering. Stuttering is a type of speech and language difficulty that leads to repetition, hesitation, and other dysfluencies that interfere with the free flow of speech and impede communication (Bishop, 1990). In the 1920s and 1930s there was a widely held theory that changing handedness and speech problems were linked.

Many of these early views were based on the Ballard study of 1912, which linked changing hand preference with stuttering. Ballard sent questionnaires to a large number of students and obtained replies from 13,189 of them. He reported that the incidence of stuttering in children whose hand preference had not been interfered with was 1.1%, but that in naturally left-handed children who had been compelled to write with their right hand it was nearly four times greater at 4.3 %.

Similar findings were also reported in handicapped children and the rate of stuttering was even more dramatic. It is reported that in children whose handedness had developed naturally the incidence of stuttering was 1.5 %, but that in children who were compelled to change their hand preference the incidence of stuttering was 19 % (Reference). Another researcher reported that

27 % of stutterers in his survey had had their handedness changed (Fagan, 1931).

According to Samuel Orton, mentioned earlier, the explanation is that forcing a child to change his or her preferred hand will interfere with the natural development of his or her brain lateralization and thereby cause confusion in the cerebral dominance which results in stuttering (Bishop, 1990).

Just before the Second World War, one researcher reported that 72% of left handed children had been compelled to change to using their right-hand and that 58% of left handed adults had been compelled to change to using their right-hand. He also reported that among people who stuttered 34% of children and 29% of adults also showed signs of ambidexterity (Bryngelson, 1939). Clearly attitudes have changed considerably since that time.

Another researcher, working with people who stuttered, found that the frequency of those with a mixed handed or left handed preference for hand, eye or foot was higher than in a control group (Morley, 1957).

Summary

A strong preference for either the right or left hand is good evidence of a normally lateralized brain and by examining Figure 1-1 it is possible to identify the specialisms that a person with such preferences should be expected to possess. Whilst there are no particular defects or conditions associated with a preference for the right hand, there are a few that are associated with a preference for the left hand, but as most of these result arise from difficulties at or around the time of birth, most of these will have been identified before the handedness of a child was identified at around at age of 6 years.

Mixed handedness, after the age of six years when preferences have matured and settled, is a strong indication that the person has an unusual symmetrical brain where the tasks are divided equally and randomly, without the specialisms developed by a lateralized brain. This arrangement is likely to have consequences on the intelligence, skills and performance of the person concerned.

Whilst it is normal for young children to experiment with both hands at most tasks in their infant years, compelling a child to switch hands is likely to have profound and, as yet, unspecified consequences. It will require a reorganization of the child's neural functioning that will produce no, as yet, identified positive consequences but will result in a number of negative effects, including stuttering.

Fortunately, the days when it was considered acceptable for teachers and parents to restrain a child by tying his or her left hand behind the back with a belt, inflicting corporal punishment for using the left hand and refusing food to children who insisted on eating it with the left hand, has passed min most countries.

However, the discrete pressures of always demonstrating a task with the right hand and of correcting errors by taking the writing implement from the child's left hand and returning it to the right hand and of providing equipment at home and at school, which is specifically designed to be used by right handers, continues widely and needs to be addressed as it can have the same effect, in as little as only a week or two.

The best way for parents and teachers to help young children is to encourage them to practice their manual skills in a relaxed atmosphere where they can discover their own preferences and to avoid the temptation to persuade, encourage or compel them to change anything. Be aware of your own conduct and the likely effect that it will have on the child. Watch the child intelligently and relate what you see to what you know and discuss any concerns that you may have with a medical practitioner.

Chapter 5

GAMES TO PLAY AT HOME

Introduction

Before attempting any of the tests, it is good practice to try a couple of quick and simple games. They help the children to relax, the adult and the child to bond, and the adult to get an idea of the likely results to be achieved in the tests.

The Kanizsa Triangle Illusion

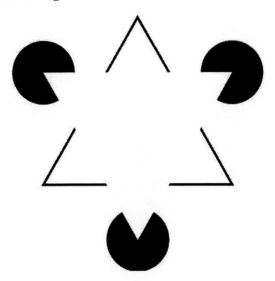

(Kanizsa, 1955)

Figure 4-1- The Kanizsa Triangle.

Strictly, there are no triangles on this page. It takes little imagination (a left handed trait) to imagine joining the black lines together to form the first triangle. It takes a little more imagination to believe that the reason for not being able to see a solid black triangle and for the areas missing from the three circles is that there is a second, white triangle superimposed on the diagram.

Understanding the Kanizsa Triangle

The Kanizsa Triangle illusion was first described in 1955 by an Italian psychologist named Gaetano Kanizsa. Gestalt use this illusion to describe the law of closure, one of the Gestalt Laws of Perceptual Organization. According to this principle, objects that are grouped together tend to be seen as being part of a whole. We tend to ignore gaps and perceive the contour lines in order to make the image appear as a cohesive whole.

Thurston's Hand Test

In this test the subject is asked to identify whether each picture shows a right or left hand. Right handers will take time and make mistakes but left handers will find the task simple and easy.

Left handers use the right hemisphere of their brains and have an ability to conceptualize size, shape and distance in three dimensions that allows them to rotate the hands and identify whether they are right or left hands.

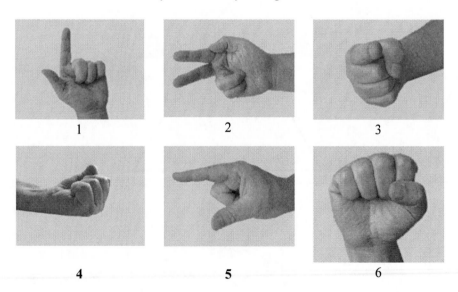

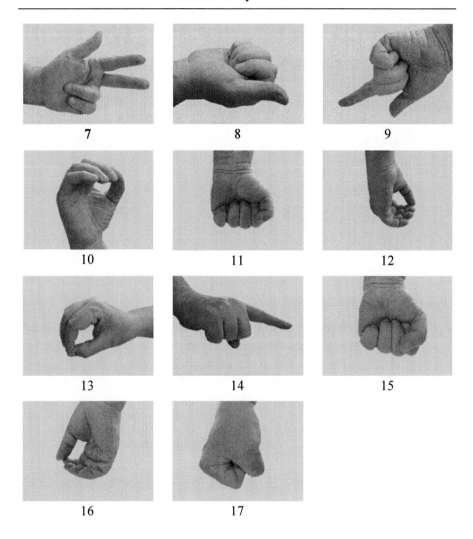

Figure 4-2- Thurston's Hand Test.

Stroop Task Online

Read the words as they are printed, from left to right in the usual way. Ignore the fact that they are printed in another color.

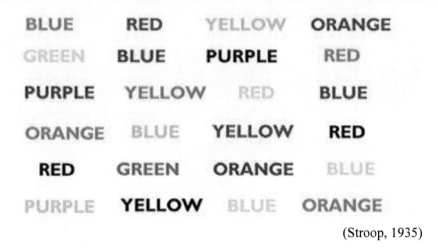

(Stroop, 1935)

Figure 4-3- Stroop Task Online.

Tapley and Bryden Handedness Measure

Using the left hand, start in the top left hand corner and work down and round the figure putting dots in every circle that you can get to in 30 seconds. Then use the right hand to start at the top right hand corner and work down and round the figure putting dots in every circle that you can get to in 30 seconds.

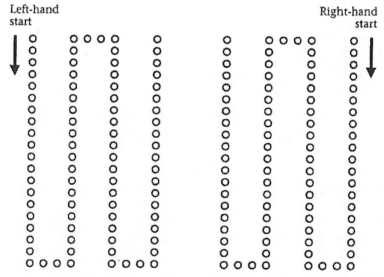

(Tapley & Bryden, 1985)

Figure 4-4- Tapley and Bryden Handedness Measure.

Chapter 6

TESTING FOR HANDEDNESS

Introduction

No record could be found of scientists ever attempting to determine whether a person is right or left handed. This is probably because, given a little time, it nearly always becomes self-evident.

For as long as any teacher that we spoke to can remember every child attending for their first day at school knew if he or she was right handed or left handed and picked up a crayon, pencil or pen instinctively with their preferred hand. They knew because using implements to scribble, trace, color, draw and write was highly valued at home and their parents spent time with them helping them to practice, demonstrating the skill to them and teaching them.

Changes to lifestyle have resulted in children now preferring to express themselves using texting, emailing and a variety of electronic keyboards, so that penmanship is now less important. When this is combined with a pressure for parents to work harder and longer to make ends meet in a deteriorating financial situation and with increasing single parent families, it is easy to see how the situation has changed.

Of course, we may hope that our failure to resolve this situation before the children went to school would be dealt with by the children's teachers at school. The problem with this is that as children have always attended school knowing if they were right or left handed, this has never been seen as a problem and therefore nobody has sought to identify a way to establish the answer quickly and effectively and nobody has ever taught the teachers how to set about the task.

A parent of left handed children recommends leaving young children in a room for ten minutes with a few sheets of paper and two pairs of school scissors, a pair of red right handed scissors and a pair of blue left handed scissors. As they are not being watched and there is nobody else in the room they can relax and experiment with the scissors, which are pretty blunt and round edged and therefore pretty safe. After the ten minutes call the child back to the group and clear up the mess. The next time that scissors are brought out the child will select either the red or blue scissors according to which ones were easier to use on the first occasion and according to which color scissors they chose you will know whether they are right or left handed. It works very well!

Having thirty children to deal with in a class is not the best way to deal with this situation. Much better for it to be dealt with on a one-to-one basis as with a parent and a child. Parents and teachers, keen for children to learn the skills required at schools are actively seeking ways to help children identify their hand choice and start to learn the skills that they need to succeed at school.

However, when difficulties with handedness arose and there was a need to assess handedness skills, scientists have frequently used a batch of tests called the WatHand Box Test. Whilst this test is widely recognized as having many strengths, it is not specifically targeted at pre-school children.

There are nine tests in the WatHand Box Test and we shall look at each in turn:

Test Number 1. Placing rings on hooks (Uni-manual)

Test Number 2. Lifting a cupboard door (Bi-manual)

Test Number 3. Picking up a candy dispenser that was behind the cupboard

Test Number 4. Using a toy hammer (Bi-manual)

Test Number 5. Tossing a ball (Uni-manual)

Test Number 6. Opening a lock with a key (Bi-manual)

Test Number 7. Using a screw driver (Uni-manual)

Test Number 8. Pushing small buttons on a gadget (e.g. a mobile 'phone) (Bi-manual)

Test Number 9. Tossing a Ball at a Target (Uni-manual)

(Bryden et al., 2000)

Specific Instructions for the administration of the individual tests in the WatHand Box Test (WBT)

Test Number 1. Placing rings on hooks (Uni-manual)

Set-up

Place a board with six hooks in a line approximately 1 inch/ 2.5cms apart on the table in front of the child so that it is accessible to both hands. Place the six rings in a horizontal row, with approximately 1 inch/ 2.5 cms between each ring. The rings should be nearer to the child than the board and accessible to both hands.

Task

At a signal from the assessor the child picks up one ring at a time and places it on a separate hook as quickly as possible. The assessor should stop timing as soon as the child has placed the last ring on a hook and released it.

Demonstration

The assessor should demonstrate the task while sitting beside the child. While demonstrating the task, emphasize:

- Use of only one hand to hold the ring;
- That the exercise is being timed and that time should not be wasted. (This is preferable to causing the child to rush and make mistakes).

Practice

Give the child one practice with each hand. A practice attempt shall consist of placing three rings on the hooks. If any fault of procedure is observed, the assessor should interrupt at the earliest opportunity and remind the child of the rules or re-demonstrate.

Trials

Both hands are tested. Allow two trials for each hand.

Record

The time taken (in seconds) to complete each trial.

Strengths of this test

This task is likely to be unlike anything that a child of this age has previously attempted, which is as it should be as these are tests of innate ability rather than of any learned skill.

Likely difficulties with this test

This is an excellent way to start the tests. None of the children that were tested in this way had any real problems with this test and so it was a convenient way to settle their nerves and get the testing under way.

The only difficulty that any of the children experienced with this task was when a few of them attempted to grip the ring tightly between their forefinger and thumb and then place the bottom of the ring over the hook, which meant that they then had to let it fall back in order to rest on the hook, which was a little awkward for them.

Test Number 2. Lifting a cupboard door   (Bi-manual)

Set-up

Place the cupboard on the table in front of the child so that it is easily accessible to both hands and the door opens up or down rather than to left or right, which would encourage the use of one or other of the hands.

Task

At a signal from the assessor the child opens the cupboard door.

Demonstration

Demonstrate the task while sitting beside the child. While demonstrating the task, emphasize:

• Use just one hand to open the door.

Practice

Give the child one practice with each hand. If any fault of procedure is observed, the assessor should interrupt at the earliest opportunity and remind the child of the rules or re-demonstrate.

Trials

The child should be allowed four attempts at this task with just enough time to break concentration between each attempt.

Record

The hand used to open the door.

Likely difficulties with this test

The ideal set-up is to have a cupboard with a single door that opens up or down. Using a double door usually results in the child opening one door and having a look inside and then opening the other door to look in that side. By having the door open up or down rather than to right or left removes the tendency to go with the door rather than to use the preferred hand.

Test Number 3. Picking up a candy dispenser that was behind the cupboard   (Bi-manual)

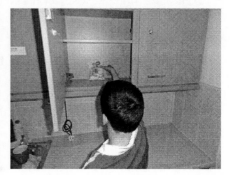

Set-up

This test is run in conjunction with the previous test. A small sweet, such as a single M & M chocolate, is concealed in the box without being seen by the child being assessed.

Task

At a signal from the assessor the child opens the cupboard door, sees the sweet and puts it in his or her mouth.

Demonstration

After demonstrating how to lift the cupboard door, the assessor simply needs to tell the child that there is a surprise in the box and that it is theirs. This allows the child to react instinctively to the chocolate, which is what is required.

Practice

The child will have already practiced opening the door and should not need to practice taking the sweet!

Trials

The child should be allowed four attempts at this task with just enough time to enjoy the sweet (and break concentration) between each attempt.

Record

The hand used to take the sweet.

Likely difficulties with this test

In this task we are attempting to understand how the child's mind is "wired" and the way that they react when not given time to think about the situation. It is for this reason that we suggest offering the child four M &M's rather than a stick of celery. The celery generally fails to extract the same reaction from the child!

Test Number 4. Using a toy hammer   (Bi-manual)

Set-up

Place the workbench on the table directly in front of the child. Place the pegs in the workbench only as far as is necessary in order for them to remain upright. Place the hammer flat on the table in the T-position so that it is easily accessible to the hand being tested.

Task

At a signal from the assessor the child picks up the hammer and hammers the pegs, one at a time, as quickly as possible into the board. The examiner should stop timing when the last peg in driven into the board.

Demonstration

Demonstrate the task while sitting beside the child. While demonstrating the task, emphasize:

- Use one hand to hold the hammer;
- Work as quickly as possible (rushing is not a problem in this test!).

Practice

Give the child one practice with each hand. If any fault of procedure is observed, the assessor should interrupt at the earliest opportunity and remind the child of the rules or re-demonstrate.

Trials

Both hands are tested. Allow two for each hand.

Record

The time taken (in seconds) to complete each trial.

Likely difficulties with this test

This is another simple test, but the children thoroughly enjoyed being able to "let-go" and bash the nail as hard as they could. The assessor needs to stay awake for this test as most children complete the task between 1 and 2 seconds, so you miss it if you blink!

Test Number 5. Tossing a ball at a Target (Uni-manual)

Setup

Place the target level with the top of the child's head.

Task

The child stands 3 feet / 1m from the target and throws the Velcro ball at the Velcro target.

Demonstration

Demonstrate the task while standing beside the child. While demonstrating the task, emphasize:

- Use one hand to hold ball;
- Hit the target.

Practice

Give the child five practices with each hand. A practice attempt shall consist of throwing the ball at the target. If any fault of procedure is observed, the assessor should interrupt at the earliest opportunity and remind the child of the rules or re-demonstrate.

Trials

Ten for each hand.

Record

Number of times the ball hits the target.

Likely difficulties with this test

Children just starting at school may not be familiar with throwing underarm and may prefer to throw overarm, but this is not a problem. Encourage them to throw in a controlled manner and to take careful aim, rather than to throw for power. Keep talking to them to assist them to maintain their focus on the task, rather than allow themselves to be easily distracted.

Test Number 6. Opening a lock with a key   (Bi-manual)

Set-up

Place the padlock and key 2 inches/ 5 cms apart in a central position in front of the child with the handle of the key nearest to the child.

Task

At a signal from the assessor the child picks up the padlock with one hand and grasps the key with the other. The child then inserts the key in the padlock and unlocks the lock as quickly as possible. The assessor should stop timing as soon as the child has unlocked the lock.

Demonstration

Demonstrate the task while sitting beside the child. While demonstrating the task, emphasize:

- Use one hand to hold the lock;
- Work as quickly as possible.

Practice

Give the child one practice with each hand. If any fault of procedure is observed, the assessor should interrupt at the earliest opportunity and remind the child of the rules or re-demonstrate.

Trials

Both hands are tested. Allow two for each hand.

Record

The time taken (in seconds) to complete each trial.

Likely difficulties with this test

This is a very good test as it requires the child to be able to conceptualize the lock and the key to decide what is required to be done in order to open the lock. All the boys and all but a handful of the girls managed to open the lock within thirty seconds, especially when prompted that they might need to turn the key around in order to make it fit the lock.

We noticed that some children attempted to swap the lock and key between hands after they started the test. Clearly, this is an indication that they prefer to use the "other" hand to the one that they were asked to use.

Problems may arise if the lock and key are dropped on the floor and the child has to chase around under the table to find the key and then bangs their head, etc. These difficulties can usually be avoided by placing the lock and key in the center of the table at the start of the test and encouraging the child to work over the center of the table.

Test Number 7. Using a screw driver   **(Uni-manual)**

Set-up

Place the workbench on the table directly in front of the child. Place the screws in the workbench only as far as is necessary in order for them to remain upright. Place the screwdriver flat on the table so that it is easily accessible to the hand being tested.

Task

The child holds the screwdriver with one hand and grasps the board with the other. At a signal the child screws the screw into the board as quickly as possible. The assessor should stop timing as soon as the child has screwed the last screw firmly into the board.

Demonstration

Demonstrate the task while sitting beside the child. While demonstrating the task, emphasize:

- Use one hand to hold the screwdriver;
- Work as quickly as possible.

Practice

Give the child one practice with each hand. If any fault of procedure is observed, the assessor should interrupt at the earliest opportunity and remind the child of the rules or re-demonstrate.

Trials

Both hands are tested. Allow two trials for each hand.

Record

The time taken (in seconds) to complete each trial.

Likely difficulties with this test

This is a skilled task and a valuable test. If the block is placed on the table and the child invited to drive the screw down into the block it is a very difficult and will take several minutes for each child and some children will fail. If the block is placed on its side on the table and the child asked to drill the screw into the block parallel to the table, it is a much simpler task and can be performed quite quickly.

Test Number 8. Pushing small buttons on a gadget (e.g. a mobile 'phone) **(Bi-manual)**

Set-up

Place the gadget on the table so that it is easily accessible to both hands.

Task

At a signal the child presses each button on the gadget as quickly as possible. The assessor should stop timing as soon as the child has pressed the last button and released it. The gadget must remain in contact with the table. The other hand may be used to hold the gadget steady.

Demonstration

Demonstrate the task while sitting beside the child. While demonstrating the task, emphasize:

- Use one hand to press the buttons;
- Work as quickly as possible.

Practice

Give the child one practice with each hand. If any fault of procedure is observed, the assessor should interrupt at the earliest opportunity and remind the child of the rules or re-demonstrate.

Trials

Both hands are tested. Allow two trials for each hand.

Record

The time taken (in seconds) to complete each trial.

Likely difficulties with this test

It had been suggested that a toy mobile telephone would be a good way to carry out this test, but this caused a lot of problems. The tests have been designed to be tests of a range of skills with which the children are unfamiliar but which are well within their ability. Unfortunately, nowadays few children are unfamiliar with mobile telephones. When pressing the buttons with the index finger was demonstrated, a large majority of the children responded by performing the task using a double thumbs technique and were unable to contemplate only using one finger to use a mobile telephone. Several children followed this with elaborate, sophisticated, imaginary calls to friends and relatives. The mobile telephone was also "lost" several times when children passing-by decided to borrow it.

The toy mobile telephone that was used lit up and made a noise when a number was pressed and this clearly pleased the children, but became a problem when the batteries became "tired" after only a few minutes of constant use and thereafter only worked occasionally. It was also found that the toys were simply made and the buttons quickly became jammed so that they did not pop back into position as they were designed to do. This too became a distraction.

It was finally decided to use a calculator that despite its low price was well made, used to constant use and with which the children had no previous experience. The calculator also allowed a quick check that all the numbers had been pressed by displaying them on the screen.

Some other simple tests

Although some people are ambidextrous and have no preference when undertaking some simple tasks, most of us are a little more choosy when it comes to using even simple tools. These are some simple tasks that have been tried with children, although care is required to ensure that none of the tools are sharp.

Test Number 10. Scribbling/ Tracing/ Coloring/ Drawing/ Writing

Set-up

Place the pen (or pencil) and paper on the table directly in front of the child.

Task

At a signal from the assessor the child picks up the pen (or pencil) and copies three words that have been written down for them to copy.

Demonstration

Demonstrate the task while sitting beside the child. While demonstrating the task, emphasize:

• Use one hand to hold the pen (or pencil);

Practice

Give the child one practice with each hand. If any fault of procedure is observed, the assessor should interrupt at the earliest opportunity and remind the child of the rules or re-demonstrate.

Trials

Both hands are tested. Allow two trials for each hand.

Record

The time taken (in seconds) to complete each trial.

Likely difficulties with this test

There should be none.

Test Number 11. Using Scissors

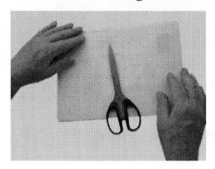 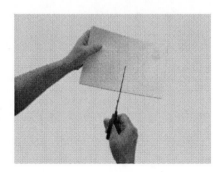

Set-up

Place the school scissors and paper on the table directly in front of the child.

Task

At a signal from the assessor the child picks up the scissors and cuts the paper in half. The assessor should stop timing when the paper has been cut in half.

Demonstration

Demonstrate the task while sitting beside the child. While demonstrating the task, emphasize:

- Use one hand to hold the scissors;
- Work as quickly as possible (rushing is not a problem in this test!).

Practice

Give the child one practice with each hand. If any fault of procedure is observed, the assessor should interrupt at the earliest opportunity and remind the child of the rules or re-demonstrate.

Trials

Both hands are tested. Allow two trials for each hand.

Record

The time taken (in seconds) to complete each trial.

Likely difficulties with this test

Some children struggle to use scissors for the first time.

Test Number 12 Slicing Toast

Set-up

Place the slice of toast and the plastic knife on the table directly in front of the child.

Task

At a signal from the assessor the child picks up the knife and cuts the toast in half. The assessor should stop timing when the toast has been cut in half.

Demonstration

Demonstrate the task while sitting beside the child. While demonstrating the task, emphasize:

- Use one hand to hold the knife;
- Work as quickly as possible (rushing is not a problem in this test!).

Practice

Give the child one practice with each hand. If any fault of procedure is observed, the assessor should interrupt at the earliest opportunity and remind the child of the rules or re-demonstrate.

Trials

Both hands are tested. Allow two for each hand.

Record

The time taken (in seconds) to complete each trial.

Likely difficulties with this test

Make sure that the knife is pretty blunt and will not cut the child!

Test Number 13. Stirring a drink

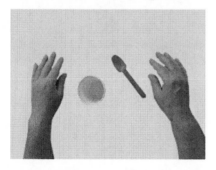 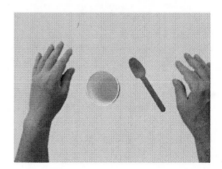

Set-up

Place the cup and spoon on the table directly in front of the child.

Task

At a signal from the assessor the child picks up the spoon and stirs the contents of the cup, twice around the cup. The examiner should stop timing when the task has been completed.

Demonstration

Demonstrate the task while sitting beside the child. While demonstrating the task, emphasize:

- Use one hand to hold the spoon;

Practice

Give the child one practice with each hand. If any fault of procedure is observed, the assessor should interrupt at the earliest opportunity and remind the child of the rules or re-demonstrate.

Trials

Both hands are tested. Allow two for each hand.

Record

The time taken (in seconds) to complete each trial.

Likely difficulties with this test

Don't put too much in the cup! Just enough for effect.

Test Number 14. Placing Pegs in peg board'

Set-up

Place the peg-board on the table-top mat in front of the child. Lay 10 pegs on the mat on the side of the board corresponding to the preferred hand. The pegs should be placed in two rows horizontal rows of five, with approximately one inch/ 2.5 cms between columns and rows. To test the other hand, reverse the position of the board and pegs.

Task

The child holds the board with one hand and grasps a peg with the other. The grasped peg must remain in contact with the mat until the child is told to begin. At a signal the child places the pegs in any of the holes in the board. The examiner should stop timing when the child releases the last peg. Both hands are tested.

Demonstration

While demonstrating the task emphasize:

- Holding the board steady;
- Picking up the pegs and inserting them one at a time;
- Using only one hand during a trial;
- Inserting the pegs in any order;
- Working as quickly as possible.

Practice

Give the child one practice attempt with each hand. A practice shall consist of the child placing 5 pegs in the board. If any fault of procedure occurs, the examiner should interrupt at the earliest opportunity and either re-demonstrate or remind the child.

Trials

Give the child two practices for each hand. Test the preferred hand first, then the other. No assistance may be given.

Record

The number of seconds taken to complete each correct trial.
Failed trial (F) if the child commits a procedural fault i.e.

- Picks up more than one peg at a time
- Changes hands or uses two hands during a trial

Test Number 15. Finger Tapping Test

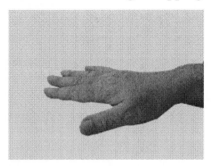 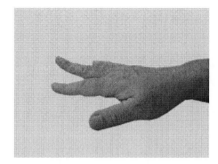

Set-up

The child is seated at a table with both feet on the floor and arms resting comfortably on the table, palms facing down.

Task

The child places the preferred hand palm down, fingers extended. At a signal the child taps the index finger as quickly as possible for thirty seconds, keeping the hand and arm stationary. Both hands are tested in an alternate fashion.

Demonstration

While demonstrating the task, emphasize:

- Palm down and fingers extended;
- Lifting the index finger quickly up and down, while tapping the surface of the table;
- Keeping the hand and arm stationary.

Practice

Give the child one practice attempt lasting 10 seconds for each hand. If any fault of procedure is observed the examiner should interrupt and give a reminder or demonstrate correct procedure.

Trials

Two for each hand.

Record

- Preferred hand.
- Number of taps.

Failed trial (F) if the child commits a procedural fault i.e. uses a different finger.

Record any unwanted movement of the limbs and other fingers.

Chapter 7

ISSUES SURROUNDING TESTING

The reason for undertaking testing is to get a result and preferably the right result. It is for this reason that the way that the testing is done is as important as the actual tests that are done.

Before any testing of children is undertaken we need to ensure that everything is legal. No testing may be undertaken without parental consent, so that if the testing is being done by the parents there is no problem. If the testing is being done at school, by teachers, then there is a presumed consent as examinations and tests and teaching children to read and write are all routine parts of a regular child's education and again there is no problem.

The other factor that we need to take into consideration before starting any testing is health and safety. We need to check that the room that is being used, the equipment that is being used and the clothing of both the person being tested and the person carrying out the testing is suitable for the purpose for which it is being used.

The tests involve the use of both a knife and a pair of scissors, but clearly these should both be of a design intended for use by children and probably made of plastic rather than metal. The board for the first test with the hooks and rings may be home made and, if it is, then it needs to be sanded to remove any splinters or sharp edges. The target in test 9 should not be placed on the back of a door, not because any person walking through the door could be hit by the soft ball, but because the child will be standing very close to the door and could be struck by anybody walking briskly through the door. The fluid in the cup in test 13 should not be tea or coffee or any other hot liquid that, if spilt, could injure the child.

When to do the tests

Keep the tests low key and do not make an issue out of them. They should be a regular part of the interaction between an adult and a child, part of having fun.

Ensure that the child is fit, healthy and alert. A child suffering with a cold or 'flu will have trouble focusing on any task.

Make sure that the child is well rested when he or she undertakes the tests as performance at this age will vary according to the time of day and the child's state of exhaustion.

Where to do the tests

Select a room where the two of you can be alone and other people can be excluded. Keep distractions to a minimum. This might mean turning off a television, radio, computer or public address system as well as your own mobile telephone. It might mean removing books or toys left on tables. You may have to close curtains if other children are playing outside the room.

Select a room with a pleasant and relaxed atmosphere, where the temperature is not too hot or too cold, where there is adequate, but not distracting lighting and no unnecessary noise. You will want the children to focus on the task in hand and not to become distracted.

The Results

Make a good record of the results of your testing. Record the full results of each of the tests achieved by the child (the objective results) and also any background information that you noticed about the way that they performed the tests (the subjective results) as these can sometimes be even more important when interpreting the results of the tests.

The author recently spent over a year testing children's handedness skills and tested over eight hundred children on the same battery of tests. Watching this number of children performing the same tests can easily become very boring and it is easy to "switch off". After packing the testing equipment into the bag after testing the last child, the Principal found one more child and testing re-started. This child managed to perform every single one of the nine tests in a way that none of the other eight hundred children had. This revitalized the author and the results were highly significant.

Reliability and validity

These two words describe the features of any test that mean that it is effective.

Reliability means that if the test is repeated several times, possibly by several different testers, at several different places, but on the same subject, then the result will always be the same or as close as to make no difference.

Validity means that the test is actually measuring what it is designed to measure.

As these tests have been designed to test the way that a child's mind works and the innate preferences of a child the problem is a complex one but one to which the best minds and the best academics have given much thought.

Dyspraxia

Any time that an adult, particularly a teacher or other specialist works with a child, he or she may become aware of problems that are being experienced by a child. All adults have a responsibility of care for a child in their care and need to report any illness, injury or developmental condition that is affecting the child, so that steps may be taken to remove the child from any danger or treat any condition. A good example of this is Dyspraxia.

Dyspraxia (otherwise known as Developmental Co-ordination Disorder (D.C.D.) or Clumsy Child Syndrome) is "an impairment or immaturity of the organization of movement. Associated with this there may be problems of language, perception and thought."

(Dyspraxia Foundation, 1998 in Boon 2002)

The condition usually comes to notice when the child first goes to school and can be easily compared with other children at the same age and stage of development and where he or she is noticed to be constantly knocking over the furniture and making a nuisance of themselves.

A teacher or other specialist noticing the symptoms of Dyspraxia should report this.

Chapter 8

IMPROVING HAND PROFICIENCY

Introduction

Today we live full, active lives, often preparing long lists of tasks that we need to achieve in order to survive, all the jobs that we should do in order to fulfill our responsibilities at work and at home and all the things that we would like to do in order to achieve happiness. A wide range of talents and skills are required in order to achieve all these objectives.

Whereas in previous centuries our ancestors succeeded by outrunning predators and successfully hunting food and therefore required great strength, speed and power in order to survive, today we are required to use small electronic tools such as mobile 'phones, laptop computers and satellite navigation equipment in order to succeed in our daily lives. We therefore require less physical prowess and greater hand proficiency than our ancestors and the recent public debate on obesity and physical activity has reflected some of the consequences of these changes.

It is interesting that whilst our legs and feet continue to perform the same old regular tasks of standing, walking and running, with occasional bursts of kicking and jumping thrown in as recreation that they have undertaken for centuries, the new skills such as writing which initially became a universal requirement but which is now being removed from school syllabuses as other skills such as using keypads and keyboards take over, have required that our arms hands and fingers have had to develop an entirely new range of skills.

The Current Situation

Human movement scientists have categorized all movement into two categories according to the size of the muscles involved, the level of control of the muscles and the aim of task:

Involuntary or reflexive movement patterns usually start during the prenatal period and continue until a year after a child's birth. Some reflexive movements are essential for a child's survival; these include breathing which starts around the time of a child's delivery and which continues throughout his or her entire life.

Voluntary movements include all the regular movements of our daily life that are under the control of the brain. This type of movement requires decision making followed by co-ordination of the neural and muscular systems in order to ensure its accurate execution.

Voluntary movements can also be classified into two types:

Fine motor skills are "those movements that need precision, accuracy and fine motor control that are almost entirely performed by small muscles such as those in the fingers, hands and wrists in activities such as writing and drawing".

Gross motor skills are "those movements that are performed with large muscle groups and for activities that need force or speed to transfer an object or absorb an object's shock". (Williams, 1983).

All voluntary movements are initiated in the brain and controlled by the brain. Impulses are then dispatched from the brain and down the spine, through what is called the Central Nervous System (C.N.S.), to the Peripheral

Nervous System (P.N.S.), which is a system of nerves that link together to form neural pathways that join the C.N.S. to the limbs and the extremities of the body. When the impulse reaches the motor nerve at which it was targeted, it innervates (activates) the muscle and causes it to contract and thereby generate movement of the joint on which the muscle acts, such as bending fingers to grasp and hold an object.

Frequently, large, dynamic, gross movements such as hammering, throwing a ball, catching an object and moving heavy objects are generated by a single large muscle which is often innervated by one or two motor nerves, whereas considerably smaller, delicate, fine movements often require many nerves to innervate the muscle and to generate the high levels of skill required to provide the accuracy and precision that is required to undertake tasks such as surgery, writing, painting, drawing and tailoring.

Fine manual (i.e. hand) skills employ the small muscle groups located in the fingers, hands and wrists, whereas gross manual skills require the larger muscle groups located in the forearms.

The Aim of This Chapter

The aim of this chapter is to identify the types of fine motor skills and gross motor skills that relate to the hand and then to introduce some exercises designed to enhance those skills. It will consider the different manual skills, the age of initiation and refinement of them, and selected exercises for fostering two handed proficiency and relate all of this to our knowledge of handedness and manual laterality.

We believe that "practice makes perfect" in enhancing skill. Any movement experience provides valuable opportunities for practicing and repeating skills that could facilitate the proficient development of manual abilities. In fact, the practice will improve the functioning of both brain (the software) and muscles (hardware), so that work more proficiently.

Fine Manual Skills

Types of Fine Manual Skills

Fine manual skills are particularly important and obvious during the infancy period (from birth to 24 months of age). It is at this stage that children develop the hand/eye co-ordination that they require in order to manipulate the variety of objects with which they come into contact.

Infant object manipulation manifests itself in a number of different ways as we learn to deal with objects of varying size, shape, texture and color. The techniques employed include reaching, grasping, releasing, object manipulation, design and form copying, finger movements, patting, axial hand movements and bimanual movements (Williams, 1983).

Reaching: This involves the child stretching his or her hand out away from his or her body towards a target object. In adults, reaching and grasping are combined into a smooth movement, called prehension, in which the adult takes control of the object. The primary actors in reaching are the arm and forearm.	
Grasping: This is where the fingers adapt to the shape of the object so as to be able to grip it and control it. Grasping is the second part of prehension. The primary actors for grasping are the wrist and fingers.	
Releasing: Having grasped an object, there clearly comes a time to release it. The child relaxes and extends the finger muscles so that the object is released. This movement helps the child to perform continuous prehension from one object to another The primary actors for releasing are the wrist and fingers.	
Object manipulation: This may be demonstrated by shaking, pulling, rubbing, squeezing, tearing or throwing the object, hitting the object on a surface, or by withholding the object when somebody else pulls it.	

Form copying: This is the ability to draw different designs and to copy specific models. It consists of drawing lines horizontally, vertically and diagonally and also variant geometric shapes such as triangles.

Finger movements: This involves the child tapping one finger onto a table or similar surface repeatedly as quickly as possible or touching each finger with his or her thumb in a sequence starting with the index finger.

Tapping: In this movement the child taps one hand onto a table or similar surface repeatedly as quickly as possible.

Axial movements: Axial movements are performed by the upper part of the hand through bending, extending, and turning the arm and forearm repeatedly.

Bimanual movements: This involves using both hands to manipulate an object in which both arms move bilaterally on the either side of the body. The actions of both hands at the same time or at different times are important for manipulating objects such as milk bottles.

Development of fine manual skills

The first attempts at reaching take place during the prenatal period when the infant instinctively moves the hand toward the mouth. After the birth the child continues to move the hand to reach for objects relying on hand/eye coordination, although many of the initial attempts are unsuccessful as the baby focuses on the hand rather the object. Brain laterality leads to the initial attempts at reaching being focused on just one favored hand.

In time, the infant learns to focus on the object and to use orientation movements by extending the arm in line with the target. Successfully moving the hand so that it comes into contact with the object usually occurs around three to fourth months of age (Piek, 2006). For successful reaching both the position of the body and the information received from the eye are important. Thus parents can facilitate successful reaching by placing the object in the infant's line of vision and by ensuring that the body position is closer to upright than to lying down.

The development of grasping is the next sequential process. The first grasping is reflexive and begins during the gestational period. Reflexive grasping continues until 8 weeks after birth. When an object is placed on the palm of the baby's hand, he or she instinctively flexes the fingers in order to grasp it. An infants' initial attempt at a voluntary grasping movement is as a form of squeezing when aged between 8 to 20 weeks when the infant flexes the fingers and bends the wrist in order to hold an object between the fingers. At an age of 28 weeks the infant can hold an object in the palm of the hand. Pincer grasping occurs at an age of 4.5 years at which time the child can use just the thumb and index finger in order to grasp and hold an object.

Researchers have identified that children move through a number of stages as they develop their object manipulation skills (Uzgiris, 1967):

Between the ages of 6 and 11 months infants begin to explore objects by shaking them and hitting them against a surface and later by tearing, pulling, squeezing, rubbing, dropping, throwing, and turning them around.

Between the ages of 11 and 18 months infants try to investigate social interaction by withholding the object from other people in order to secure and explore their reaction.

At about 1 year of age, children develop the ability to copy and draw different designs and begin to display this in the form of scribbling. They start to display other movement expressions that are unrelated to any goal or visual model.

From 18 to 24 months children classify and label objects verbally.

At the age of 3 years a child begins to pay attention to the characteristics of visual models that are presented to him or her for copying.

Between the ages of 4 and 5 years children start to use lines, angles and smooth contours in their drawing. Most children are able to draw different geometric shapes from the age of 6 years.

Finger movements begin to develop between the ages of 5 and 7 years. Children demonstrate different forms of finger movements such as tapping with one finger repeatedly and also touching the thumb and index fingers. Interestingly, the right hand is superior to the left hand at finger tapping but there is no difference between the right and left hands in the finger touching.

From the age of 5 years hand patting starts to develop and then gradually develops until the age of 10 years. The right hand is slightly superior to the left hand at this.

From the age of 5 years axial hand movements also develop and gradually improve until the age of 10 years. Again the right hand is slightly superior to the left hand in turning and bending/ extending the arm and forearm movements.

Researchers have suggested that bimanual coordination skills start to develop in the second year of life, but adult patterns of performance cannot be observed before 6 years of age (Birtles et al., 2001). Other researchers have reported that the development of bimanual movements as a form of smooth and skillful integration of both hands in a simple movement such as clapping occurs between 4 and 6 years of age (Ayres, 1978). The significant change in bimanual movement occurs between 5 and 6 ages but until 6.5 years the change is gradual and slight.

In the following pages we present some activities for infants and children designed to stimulate the fine manual skills that they will require for daily living (Chambers & Sugden, 2006; Nash-Wrotham & Hunt, 2003). Adults supervising such activities should be careful not to encourage the child to use one particular hand over another or to use both hands simultaneously, but to allow the child to develop naturally at his or her own pace.

Activity 1:

The coin game

Equipment required:

Twelve small coins, twelve large coins, an empty water bottle (1 pint/500ml)

Target manual skills:

Reaching, grasping and releasing

Procedure:

Lay the small coins on the table in four rows of three, so that the head side is showing.
Tell the child to turn the coins over and put them down in the same place. Repeat the procedure using the other hand. Time both hands and then repeat the task using the small coins.

Variety:

Lay the large coins on the table in four rows of three, so that the head side is showing and the coins are 1 inch/ 2.5 cm apart on the table.
Tell the child to hold the bottle upright in one hand and post the coins into the bottle as quickly as possible with other hand. Repeat the procedure using the other hand. Time both hands and then repeat the task using the small coins.

Progression:

Record the child's scores for each activity on the score sheet (Appendix 1) in order to follow the progression over a period of time.

Activity 2:

The card game

Equipment required:

A pack of playing cards

Target manual skills:

Reaching, grasping, releasing and axial movements

Procedure:

Lay any twelve cards flat on the table. Tell the child to turn them over quickly using one hand. Repeat the procedure using the other hand. Time both hands.

Variety:

Lay any twenty four cards flat on the table. Instruct the child to use both hands to turn the cards over.

Tell the child to hold the pack in one hand and deal cards with the other. Repeat the procedure using the other hand. Count the number of cards that the child deals from each hand in one minute.

Progression:

Record the child's scores for each activity on the score sheet (Appendix 1) in order to follow the progression over a period of time.

Activity 3:

Bubble wrap pop

Equipment required:

A sheet of bubble wrap

Target manual skill:

Finger movements

Procedure:

Instruct the child to burst as many bubbles as possible in one minute, using a pincer grip to grip each bubble between the finger and thumb. Repeat the procedure using the other hand.

Progression:

Record the child's scores for each activity on the score sheet (Appendix 1) in order to follow the progression over a period of time.

Activity 4:

Pass the water bottle

Equipment required:

A water bottle

Target manual skills:

Reaching, grasping, releasing and axial movements

Procedure:

The child holds the bottle in one hand. Then tell the child to release the bottle with one hand and grasp it with other and repeat the procedure for ten repetitions. Then tell the child to try to do it behind his or her back.

Progression:

Record the child's scores for each activity on the score sheet (Appendix 1) in order to follow the progression over a period of time.

Activity 5:

Peg power

Equipment required:

Pegs, tweezers, wide necked jar

Target manual skills:

Reaching, grasping, releasing and axial movements

Procedure:

Lay twelve pegs flat on the table. Tell the child to unscrew the lid of the jar and hold it steady with one hand, using tweezers to pick up the pegs one by one and drop them into the jar. Repeat the procedure using the other hand. Time each hand.

Progression:

Record the child's scores for each activity on the score sheet (Appendix 1) in order to follow the progression over a period of time.

Activity 6:

Spot the dot

Equipment required:

Felt tip pen, dotty papers (Appendices 2 , 3)

Target manual skills:

Drawing and form copying

Procedure:

Use the felt tip pen and dotty paper 1. Draw a dot on top of each of the printed dots on the page. Repeat the procedure using the other hand. Repeat the procedure using dotty paper 2.Repeat the procedure using the other hand. Score the accurate dotting.

Progression:

Record the child's scores for each activity on the score sheet (Appendix 1) in order to follow the progression over a period of time.

Activity 7:

Draw circles

Equipment required:

Felt tip pen, blank paper

Target manual skills:

Drawing and form copying

Procedure:

Give the child the pen and paper. Tell the child to draw a circle and as they do so say, "Round and stop" to stop them going over the circle again and again. Repeat this until the child has covered the paper with circles of different sizes. Assess the child's performance for the roundness of the circle and neatness and award a score out of ten.

Progression:

Record the child's scores for each activity on the score sheet (Appendix 1) in order to follow the progression over a period of time.

Activity 8:

Balloons

Equipment required:

Felt tip pen, balloon paper (Appendix 4), blank paper

Target manual skills:

Drawing and form copying

Procedure:

Give the child the pen and balloon paper. Tell the child to draw over the balloons on the balloon paper carefully and accurately. Then when the child has finished this, tell him or her to color the balloons. Assess the child's performance for the roundness of the circle and neatness and award a score out of ten.

Then give the child the pen and blank paper and tell him or her to draw balloons on the blank paper. Assess the child's performance for the roundness of the circle and neatness and award a score out of ten.

Progression:

Record the child's scores for each activity on the score sheet (Appendix 1) in order to follow the progression over a period of time.

Activity 9:

Crosses and Kisses

Equipment required:

Felt tip pen, blank paper

Target manual skills:

Drawing and form copying

Procedure:

Give the child the pen and paper. Using the felt tip pen, draw a (+) for the child on the paper. Tell the child to copy your shape and to cover the paper with crosses. Assess the child's performance for whether the arms of the (+) are the same length and score the number of correct crosses in one minute.

Give the child the pen and paper. Using the felt tip pen, draw a (x) for the child on the paper. Tell the child to copy your shape and to cover the paper with kisses. Assess the child's performance for whether the arms of the (x) are the same length and score the number of correct kisses in one minute.

Progression:

Record the child's scores for each activity on the score sheet (Appendix 1) in order to follow the progression over a period of time.

Activity 10:

Diagonals

Equipment required:

Felt tip pen, "It is raining" papers 1 and 2 (Appendices 5, 6)

Target manual skills:

Drawing and form copying

Procedure:

Give the child the pen and the "It is raining" paper 1. Tell the child to make the rain very heavy by drawing over the lines with the pen and to press hard on the paper. Then instruct the child to draw in some smaller drops of rain in between the bigger diagonals. Assess the child's performance for the number of lines drawn parallel to the rain on the printed page.

Give the child the pen and the "It is raining" paper 2. Tell the child to make the rain very heavy by drawing over the lines with the pen and to press hard on the paper. Then instruct the child to draw in some smaller drops of rain in between the bigger diagonals. Assess the child's performance for the number of lines drawn parallel to the rain on the printed page.

Progression:

Record the child's scores for each activity on the score sheet (Appendix 1) in order to follow the progression over a period of time.

Activity 11:

Squares

Equipment required:

Felt tip pen, blank paper

Target manual skills:

Drawing and form copying

Procedure:

Give the child the pen and paper. Draw a square on the paper and tell the child to copy it. Instruct the child to draw more squares until the paper is covered with squares of different sizes. Assess the child's performance for the shape of the square and score those of an acceptable standard.

Progression:

Record the child's scores for each activity on the score sheet (Appendix 1) in order to follow the progression over a period of time.

Activity 12:

Triangles

Equipment required:

Felt tip pen, "Triangle trees" (Appendix 7), blank paper

Target manual skills:

Drawing and form copying

Procedure:

Give the child the pen and paper. Draw a triangle

on the paper and tell the child to copy it. Instruct the child to draw more triangles until the paper is covered with triangles of different sizes. Assess the child's performance for the shape of the triangles and score those of an acceptable standard.

Give the child the pen and the "Triangle Trees" paper. Instruct the child to draw over the trees and then to add more trees to the page of differing sizes. Assess the child's performance for the shape of the triangles and score those of an acceptable standard completed in one minute.

Progression:

Record the child's scores for each activity on the score sheet (Appendix 1) in order to follow the progression over a period of time.

Activity 13:

Cut circles

Equipment required:

Felt tip pen, blank paper, scissors

Target manual skills:

Finger movements

Procedure:

Use the felt tip pen to draw small, medium and large circles on the paper. Instruct the child to use the scissors to cut the circles out one by one. The scissors should cut the lines accurately. Instruct the child to cut some circles clockwise and others counter- clockwise. Assess the child's performance for the accuracy of cutting and score the number of an acceptable standard.

Progression:

Record the child's scores for each activity on the score sheet (Appendix 1) in order to follow the progression over a period of time.

Activity 14:

Squeezing the sponge

Equipment required:

A sponge, a plastic bag, a tennis ball and some sand

Target manual skill:

Finger movements

Procedure:

Get the child to hold a sponge in one hand and instruct him or her to try to squeeze it and hold this position for five seconds. Repeat the procedure using the other hand
Now make the sponge wet in order to make the task more difficult. Instruct the child to squeeze the wet sponge and try to remove all water inside it. Then repeat the task with the other hand.

Variety:

Get the child to repeat the exercise with a bag of sand and a tennis ball in order to increase the difficulty of the task.

Progression:

Record the child's scores for each activity on the score sheet (Appendix 1) in order to follow the progression over a period of time.

Activity 15:

Fingertip touch

Equipment required:

A sheet of paper

Target manual skill:

Finger movements

Procedure:

Instruct the child to hold the paper between the thumb and index finger of one hand without dropping it or using the other hand. Repeat the procedure using the other hand

Then tell the child to hold the paper between the thumb and middle finger without dropping it or using the other hand. Repeat the procedure using the other hand

Then tell the child to hold the paper between the thumb and ring finger without dropping it or using the other hand. Repeat the procedure using the other hand

Then tell the child to hold the paper between the thumb and little finger without dropping it or using the other hand. Repeat the procedure using the other hand

Then work back to the index finger again.

Record the time taken to move from index finger to little finger and back to the index finger.

Progression:

Record the child's scores for each activity on the score sheet (Appendix 1) in order to follow the progression over a period of time.

Activity 16:

Dropping the ruler

Equipment required:

A plastic ruler (12 inches/25 cms)

Target manual skills:

Grasping, releasing, bimanual movement

Procedure:

Tell the child to hold the ruler vertically between the thumb and index finger of one hand. Instruct the child to place the other hand 1 inch/ 2.5 cms below the bottom of the ruler so that as he or she drops the ruler with the one hand he or she can catch it in the other hand. Then change hands and repeat the task.
Record the number of successful transfers of the ruler in one minute.

Progression:

Record the child's scores for each activity on the score sheet (Appendix 1) in order to follow the progression over a period of time.

Activity 17:

Flicking ball

Equipment required:

A ping pong ball and a sheet of paper

Target manual skill:

Finger movements

Procedure:

Put the ball on the table. Tell the child to flick the ball as far as possible with one or more of the fingers of one hand. Change hand and repeat the task. Record the distances achieved by each hand in one minute.

Variety:

Please a cup or piece of paper down 6 feet/ two meters from the ball and use it as a target, so that the child scores when the ball strikes the target.

Progression:

Record the child's scores for each activity on the score sheet (Appendix 1) in order to follow the progression over a period of time.

Activity 18:

Building books

Equipment required:

Ten books of different sizes

Target manual skill:

Reaching, grasping, releasing and finger movements

Procedure:

Put five books flat on the table on either side of the child. Instruct the child to pick up one book from one of the piles and, using just one hand, put it on top of the other pile. Repeat the task until there is one pile of ten books.
Repeat the activity using the other hand.

Progression:

Record the child's scores for each activity on the score sheet (Appendix 1) in order to follow the progression over a period of time.

Activity 19:

Finger painting

Equipment required:

3"× 3" (8cm x 8cm) plastic box, sands

Target manual skill:

Form copying

Procedure:

Fill a square plastic box with sand. Get the child to draw in the sand using their thumb. They can draw:
A circle;
A square;
A triangle;
A tree;
A boy;
A girl.
The adult should encourage the child to rub out each drawing before starting the next one.

Progression:

Record the child's scores for each activity on the score sheet (Appendix 1) in order to follow the progression over a period of time.

Activity 20:

Pushing the wall

Equipment required:

None

Target manual skill:

Axial movements

Procedure:

Instruct the child to stand approximately arm's length away from a wall. Tell the child to push against the wall with straight elbows and to hold the position for five seconds. Repeat the task three times with a five seconds rest between attempts.

Progression:

Record the child's scores for each activity on the score sheet (Appendix 1) in order to follow the progression over a period of time.

Activity 21:

Passing Beanbag

Equipment required:

A beanbag

Target manual skills:

Bimanual movement, grasping and axial movement

Procedure:

Get the child to hold a beanbag in one hand.

Then tell the child to pass it to the other hand in front of the body. Then tell the child to pass it back to the other hand in front of the body. Count the number of passes between the two hands in one minute.

Variety:

Get the child to lay down on his or her back on the floor and hold the beanbag in one hand near the leg. Then tell the child to pass the bean bag to the left hand and to catch it with left hand. Repeat if for one minute. Count the number of successful passing between the two hands.

Progression:

Record the child's scores for each activity on the score sheet (Appendix 1) in order to follow the progression over a period of time.

Activity 22:

Finger-hand control

Equipment required:

A tennis ball

Target manual skill:

Grasping and finger movements

Procedure:

Tell the child to hold the ball in the palm of one hand and to slightly squeeze the ball.
Then instruct the child to open the fingers until the ball move to the finger tips. Then to close the fingers again so that the ball comes back up so that the child can squeeze it again.
Change hands and repeat the task.

Record the number of times the child opens and closes the palm in one minute.

Progression:

Record the child's scores for each activity on the score sheet (Appendix 1) in order to follow the progression over a period of time.

Activity 23:

Rod finger movements

Equipment required:

A plastic rod, 15 inch/35 cm long

Target manual skills:

Grasping and finger movements

Procedure:

Get the child to hold the rod with both hands (2 inch/ 5 cm apart) so that the thumbs are below the rod and the fingers above it. Tell the child to hold the rod at shoulder level with the upper arms remaining at the side of the body, elbows flexed and close to the body. The rod is held by the fingertips.

Instruct the child to try to take the index fingers away from the rod, then put them back on to the rod. Repeat the task, with the middle fingers, the ring fingers and the little fingers. The key factor in this activity is that the rod should keep in horizontal and shoulder level position all the time.

Record the time taken to remove each of the fingers on the hand.

Progression: Record the child's scores for each activity on the score sheet (Appendix 1) in order to follow the progression over a period of time.	

Gross Manual Skills

Types of Gross Manual Skills

Gross manual skills belong to fundamental movement patterns that are characteristic of the childhood period from 3 to 7 years of age. Their development is dependent on both maturation and practice. The development of gross skills is a prerequisite for the acquisition of more specific movement patterns in later life, such as the functional abilities required for daily living e.g. job skills, sport skills and recreational skills. Therefore, difficulties in maturation or a lack of sufficient movement experience could result in an inability to acquire fundamental gross skills.

These situations may affect those children who suffer from specific developmental disorders for any reason or for children in big cities who do not have sufficient time or space to practice gross movements during their developmental period.

Gross manual skills include throwing, catching, striking, bouncing, and volleying.

Throwing: Throwing is the use of one hand to project an object away from the body into space. The technique used may be overarm, underarm or sidearm. Successful throwing requires the application of force along the selected trajectory. Throwing may be performed for distance or for accuracy.	

Catching: Successful catching requires the co-ordination of hand and eye to track the moving object in space, an assessment of the size and speed of the object and the co-ordination and correct positioning of the hands in order to stop and control the object.

Striking: Striking is a form of manual skill in which an object is projected by contact with an implement such as a bat or racket, etc. The skill can be executed in a number of different ways depending on the incoming trajectory of the object. These techniques include sidearm, underhand, and overhand strikes. Success in striking an object is dependent on hand/ eye co-ordination.

Bouncing: Bouncing is the ability of the hand to control the ball by pushing it down onto the ground every time that it rebounds off the ground. It requires a delicate control of force and trajectory in order to absorb the shock of ball as it rises and to exert appropriate force in order to propel the ball down again.

Volleying (as in Volleyball): This is the only gross manual skill that requires both hands to work together. Volleying is the use of both hands in a bilateral and co-ordinated movement to project a ball toward a target. The delicacy and skills required in this movement are clearly observable in a Volleyball game.

Development of Gross Manual Skills

The initial stage of throwing is observable in infancy when a child first releases an object held in his or her hand and allows it to fall to the floor (Williams, 1983). This most simple form of throwing uses only the fingers, with no contribution yet from the arm, shoulder, trunk, hips or legs. Clearly, as all these other, larger, stronger muscle groups start to contribute to the throw, the object will travel much further.

Before being selected to compete at the Olympic Games in the Javelin Throw, our young athlete will have to pass through a number of stages as he or she attempts to use more and more of the muscle groups in the body to propel the object further and further. As frustration builds at the lack of distance generated by the fingers, the muscles controlling the wrist, and then the elbow, and then the shoulder are quickly introduced to the throwing action.

It will take a few years for the developing thrower to use the trunk to propel the object and to realize that walking and running forward will assist him or her to throw further. Full extension of the toe, ankle, knee, hip, shoulder, elbow, wrist and fingers may require advanced coaching and repetitious training and even some strength training to develop all the muscles necessary to achieve their full potential and this is unlikely to occur until the mid -teens.

But throwing may also be developed in order to achieve greater accuracy. This will require coordination of hand and eye in order to ensure that the object strikes even a stationery target. In order to successfully strike a moving object it will be necessary to track that moving object in order to identify the speed and direction of movement and to anticipate the object's anticipated future trajectory so as to place the object being thrown in the position necessary to intersect that trajectory and therefore to strike the target.

Few baseball players or cricketers are capable of undertaking the necessary calculations on paper that are required to eliminate an opponent, yet many are able to instantly perform the necessary calculations in their head whilst coping with the pressure of a competitive match and a large crowd and at the same time as executing the ultimate throw in order to dispatch an opponent.

The critical period of throwing is between 3 and 7 years of age. By acquiring the basic throwing skill, the child is able to use it in different forms such as throwing underarm, sidearm and eventually overarm, according to the environmental demands. Throwing is one of the fundamental gross movement patterns for many sports such as baseball, basketball, football, handball, cricket, rugby, and athletics.

Catching a ball is a form of gross manual skill that can be executed by means of one or both hands, depending on the size of the ball. The development of catching with both hands is also an incremental process. In the initial stage the child uses the upper arms to trap the ball as they provide a larger contact area with the ball. For this reason successful catching is rare. Then, the child adjusts his or her hands according to the direction and speed of the ball, and will get his or her hands to the ball but then drop it due to stiffness in the finger muscles.

In the advanced stage, the child completely adjusts his or her body position so as to successfully catch the ball. The fingers are more active at this stage and the movement is performed with more coordination and control. The judgment necessary to catch the ball has been developed in training based on previous successful experience. Most children aged 5 years are able to demonstrate an advanced form of catching, which will prove useful in sports such as basketball, handball, cricket, and rugby where catching is very important.

Initial attempts to strike an object with a bat or racket occur at the age of 3 years. The child will use both hands if the bat or racket is heavy and one hand if it is not. Developmental changes in the striking pattern include using trunk rotation and backswing in order to increase the amplitude of the stroke. In fact in the initial stage the child seldom uses the trunk for striking and the hand movement begins from the front of the body. In addition hand movement is limited to the elbow.

Gradually, the child uses the complete rotation in the trunk first in the opposite direction of the projected ball and after strike in the same direction of the forward swing to complete the follow-through action. Besides, involvement of shoulders will be increased that results in the child produce more force to achieve farther distance. The legs use for control the balance and force production. At the age of 5 years the child could show the advanced form of striking. This movement pattern is important in cricket, baseball, and in racket sports such as tennis, table tennis, badminton, and squash.

The development of skills in ball bouncing start when a ball is dropped for the first time and starts to bounce. From this single bounce the child attempts to tap the ball repeatedly. Control of the ball is not easy until the child learns to place the hands in relation to the center of the ball. In addition the child must meet the ball as it rebounds from the floor, maintaining contact with it as long as possible while the arm pushes the ball back toward the floor. The initial forms are without co-ordination and appropriate timing of the arm action in relation to the rebound of the ball.

Advanced bouncing is performed with the wrist and fingers rather than the arm and forearm. The child could shows the advanced form at the age of 5 years and the successful bouncing is repeated successively. The ball bouncing is an important skill in sports like basketball and handball.

Movement Experiences for Gross Manual Proficiency

In the following we present some movement activities for children in order to stimulate their gross manual skills in daily living. Notice that we do not encourage the child to use both hands. Observe the movement and find which hand is better and then try to strengthen the dominant hand.

Activity 1: Ball juggling **Equipment required:** Two tennis balls **Target manual skills:** Throwing and catching	

Procedure:

Get the child to stand holding a tennis ball in the right hand. Instruct the child to throw the ball up a few inches and catch it with the same hand and then repeat this ten times. Tell the child to change hands and then repeat the task.
Record the time taken to complete the task with each hand.

Variety:

Get the child to stand holding a tennis ball in the right hand. Instruct the child to throw the ball up a few inches and catch it with the left hand and then repeat this ten times. Tell the child to change hands and then repeat the task.
Record the time taken to complete the task with each hand.
Next, get the child to stand holding a tennis ball in each hand. Instruct the child to throw both balls up a few inches and catch them with the same hand and then repeat this ten times.
Record the time taken to complete the task with each hand.
Next, get the child to stand holding a tennis ball in each hand. Instruct the child to throw both balls up a few inches and catch them with the other hand and then repeat this ten times.
Record the time taken to complete the task with each hand.

Progression:

Record the child's scores for each activity on the score sheet (Appendix 1) in order to follow the progression over a period of time.

Activity 2:

The wall game

Equipment required:

One tennis ball and a piece of chalk

Target manual skills:

Throwing and catching

Procedure:

Child stands in front of a wall 6 feet/2 meters away, holding a ball in the right hand. Instruct the child.to throw the ball against the wall in an underarm style and then catch it with the same hand and repeat this ten times. Tell the child to change hands and then repeat the task.

Record the time taken to complete the task with each hand.

Repeat the task using an overarm style.

Variety:

Draw a vertical line down the wall to separate the right and left sides. Instruct the child to throw the ball with the right hand against the left side of the wall and catch it with the right hand and repeat this ten times.

Tell the child to change hands and then repeat the task.

Progression:

Record the child's scores for each activity on the score sheet (Appendix 1) in order to follow the progression over a period of time.

Activity 3:

Throwing a beanbag at a target

Equipment required:

One beanbag, a basket, a tennis ball or a soft ball

Target manual skill:

Throwing

Procedure:

Place the basket on the ground. Get the child to stand 5 feet/ 1.5 meters away from the basket, holding the beanbag in the right hand. Instruct the child to throw the beanbag into the basket ten times. Tell the child to change hands and then repeat the task.
Get the child to repeat the task, swapping hands between each effort.

Variety:

Vary the distance and angle of the basket and the throwing technique to overarm or underarm.

Progression:

Record the child's scores for each activity on the score sheet (Appendix 1) in order to follow the progression over a period of time

Activity 4:

Bowling

Equipment required:

Seven tennis balls or other soft balls

Target manual skill:

Throwing

Procedure:

Draw a line 30 inch/85cm long and put six balls on it (3 inch/ 8cm apart). Get the child to stand behind the line 10 feet/ 3 meters away, holding a ball in one hand. Instruct the child to bowl the ball along the ground towards the first ball on the line. Instruct the child to recover the ball and bowl again, working along the balls on the line. Tell the child to change hands and then repeat the task.
Count the number of successful throws.
Get the child to repeat the task, swapping hands between each effort.

Variety:

Increase the distance between the child and the line.

Progression:

Record the child's scores for each activity on the score sheet (Appendix 1) in order to follow the progression over a period of time.

Activity 5:

Bouncing a ball

Equipment required:

One basketball or other 10 inch/ 25cm inflated ball

Target manual skill:

Bouncing

Procedure:

Get the child to stand and hold the ball in one hand. Instruct the child to use one hand to bounce the ball on the ground for one minute. Then tell the child to change hands and repeat the task.

Count the number of successful attempts in a row for one minute.

Get the child to repeat the task, swapping hands between each bounce.

Progression:

Record the child's scores for each activity on the score sheet (Appendix 1) in order to follow the progression over a period of time.

Activity 6:

Bouncing two balls

Equipment required:

Two basketball or other 10 inch/ 25cm inflated balls

Target manual skill:

Bouncing

Procedure:

Get the child to stand holding a ball in each hand. Instruct the child to bounce both balls at the same time for one minute
Count the number of successful attempts in a row.

Progression:

Record the child's scores for each activity on the score sheet (Appendix 1) in order to follow the progression over a period of time.

Activity 7:

Seated ball bouncing

Equipment required:

One basketball or other 10 inch/ 25cm inflated ball

Target manual skill:

Bouncing

Procedure:

Get the child to sit on the floor and hold the ball

in one hand. Instruct the child to use one hand to bounce the ball on the ground for one minute. Then tell the child to change hands and repeat the task.

Count the number of successful attempts in a row for one minute.

Get the child to repeat the task, swapping hands between each bounce.

Progression:

Record the child's scores for each activity on the score sheet (Appendix 1) in order to follow the progression over a period of time.

Activity 8:

Seated two ball bouncing

Equipment required:

Two basketballs or other 10 inch/ 25cm inflated balls

Target manual skill:

Bouncing

Procedure:

Get the child to sit on the floor holding a ball in each hand. Instruct the child to bounce both balls at the same time for one minute

Count the number of successful attempts in a row.

Progression:

Record the child's scores for each activity on the score sheet (Appendix 1) in order to follow the progression over a period of time.

Activity 9:

Walking along and bouncing a ball

Equipment required:

One basketball or other 10 inch/ 25cm inflated ball

Target manual skill:

Bouncing

Procedure:

Draw a 30 foot/ 10 meter line on the floor or put a long rope on the floor. Get the child to stand and hold the ball in one hand. Instruct the child to use one hand to bounce the ball on the ground as he or she walks along the line for one minute. Then tell the child to change hands and repeat the task.

Count the number of successful attempts in a row for one minute.

Get the child to repeat the task, swapping hands between each bounce.

Progression:

Record the child's scores for each activity on the score sheet (Appendix 1) in order to follow the progression over a period of time.

Activity 10:

Striking the ball

Equipment required:

One table tennis ball, one table tennis bat, one long piece of string, one roll of adhesive tape

Target manual skill:

Striking

Procedure:

Attach the ball to the string using the adhesive tape and suspend it from a tree or other suitable object so that the ball is suspended at the height of the child's chest. Instruct the child to hold the bat in one hand and to strike the ball as often as possible for one minute. Do not give the child any further instructions but allow him or her to develop his or her own pattern of movement.
Tell the child to change hands and then repeat the task.
Count the number of successful attempts in one minute.

Variety:

After a few trials, you can start to gently vary the flight of the ball.
Tell the child to change hands and then repeat the task.
Count the number of successful attempts in one minute.

Progression:

Record the child's scores for each activity on the score sheet (Appendix 1) in order to follow the progression over a period of time.

Activity 11:

Wall Tennis

Equipment required:

One table tennis ball, one table tennis bat

Target manual skill:

Striking

Procedure:

Get the child to stand 6 feet/ 2 meters away from a wall and stand facing it. Instruct the child to throw the ball gently against the wall and use the bat to hit the ball back against the wall as often as possible for one minute.
Tell the child to change hands and then repeat the task.
Count the number of successful attempts.

Progression:

Record the child's scores for each activity on the score sheet (Appendix 1) in order to follow the progression over a period of time.

Activity 12:

Keepy Uppy

Equipment required:

One table tennis ball, one table tennis bat,

Target manual skill:

Striking

Procedure:

Get the child to stand holding the bat in one hand. Instruct the child to gently drop the ball onto the bat and to use the bat to keep the ball up off the ground for one minute. Advise the child not to let the ball go to high.

Tell the child to change hands and then repeat the task.

Count the number of successful attempts.

Variety:

Child can move between forehand and backhand between sets and later between each strike.

Tell the child to change hands and then repeat the task.

Count the number of successful attempts.

Progression:

Record the child's scores for each activity on the score sheet (Appendix 1) in order to follow the progression over a period of time.

Activity 13:

Volleying

Equipment required:

One volley ball or other average sized inflated ball.

Target manual skill:

Volleying

Procedure:

Get the child to stand holding the ball with two hands. Instruct the child to gently throw the ball

in the air and using a volleyball stance to keep the ball off the ground for one minute. Advise the child not to let the ball go to high.
Tell the child to change hands and then repeat the task.
Count the number of successful attempts.

Progression:

Record the child's scores for each activity on the score sheet (Appendix 1) in order to follow the progression over a period of time.

Activity 14:

Wall volleying

Equipment required:

One volley ball or other average sized inflated ball.

Target manual skill:

Volleying

Procedure:

Get the child to stand 6 feet/ 2 meters away from the wall and stand facing it. Tell the child to gently throw the ball against the wall and to use a volleyball stance to keep the ball off the ground for one minute by bouncing it against the wall. Advise the child not to let the ball go to high.
Tell the child to change hands and then repeat the task.
Count the number of successful attempts.

Variety:

Vary the speed of the ball (slow or fast), the

distance to the wall (near or far), the direction of the wall (right or left or center) and the height of the ball (high, average, low). **Progression:** Record the child's scores for each activity on the score sheet (Appendix 1) in order to follow the progression over a period of time.	

Summary

Children are born as babies, incapable of surviving without assistance. They grow and develop naturally, but they need to undertake vigorous exercise in order to reach anything like their full potential. Provided with a suitable, interesting environment they will happily play all day and provide themselves with all the exercise that they need to fulfill that potential. As adults, we need to provide a safe environment and ample liquid refreshment and avoid any pressure or undue encouragement.

Any movement experience will provide a valuable opportunity to practice skills that facilitate the proficient development of the child's manual abilities. These abilities will include fine manual skills and gross manual skills and, as adults, we may need to check the range of skills practiced by using the lists above, which have been designed to demonstrate and test the full range of skills required for a complete development of a child.

Chapter 9

SO YOU'RE LEFT HANDED!

With almost six times as many people right handed than left handed, you are part of an exclusive club! There are many, very successful left handed people and a search of the internet will provide you with long lists of them. Here is a list of one hundred of the most interesting left handed people:

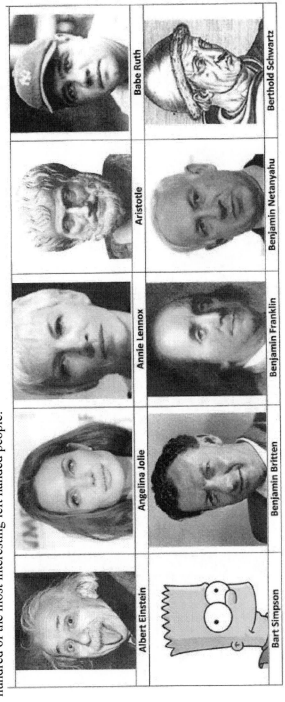

| Albert Einstein | Angelina Jolie | Annie Lennox | Aristotle | Babe Ruth |
| Bart Simpson | Benjamin Britten | Benjamin Franklin | Benjamin Netanyahu | Berthold Schwartz |

Geoffrey K. Platt, Mohsen Shafizadeh and Gordon Revolta

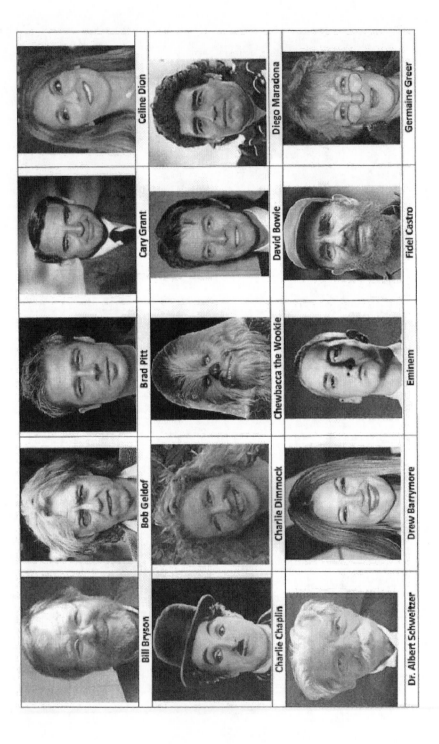

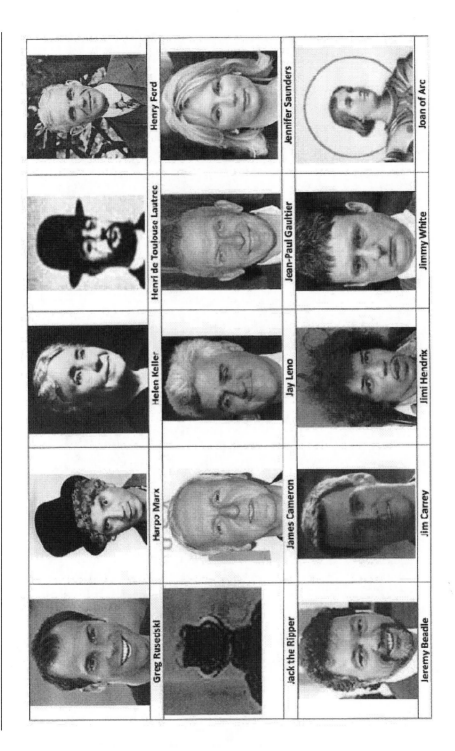

Greg Rusedski

Jack the Ripper

Jeremy Beadle

Harpo Marx

James Cameron

Jim Carrey

Helen Keller

Jay Leno

Jimi Hendrix

Henri de Toulouse Lautrec

Jean-Paul Gaultier

Jimmy White

Henry Ford

Jennifer Saunders

Joan of Arc

Geoffrey K. Platt, Mohsen Shafizadeh and Gordon Revolta

John McEnroe	Jonathan Ross	Judy Garland	Julia Roberts	Julian Clary
Juliet Morris	Julius Caesar	Keanu Reeves	Kenneth Branagh	Kim Basinger
Kurt Cobain	Leonardo Da Vinci	Lewis Carroll	Lisa Kudrow	Lord Baden-Powell

Geoffrey K. Platt, Mohsen Shafizadeh and Gordon Revolta

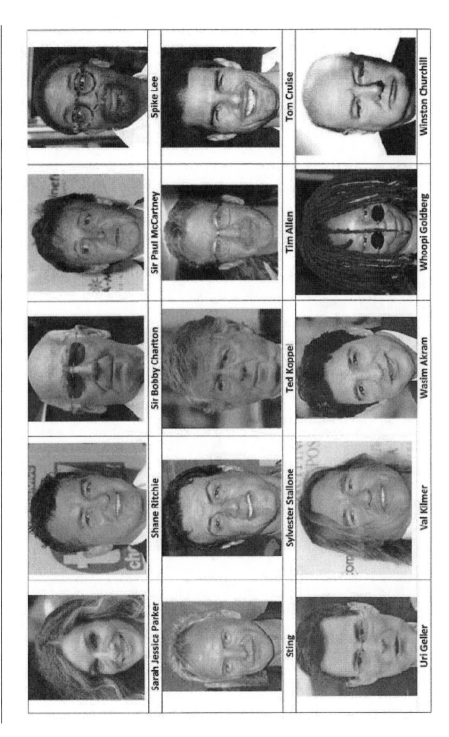

Sarah Jessica Parker

Shane Ritchie

Sir Bobby Charlton

Sir Paul McCartney

Spike Lee

Sting

Sylvester Stallone

Ted Koppel

Tim Allen

Tom Cruise

Uri Geller

Val Kilmer

Wasim Akram

Whoopi Goldberg

Winston Churchill

Five out of the last Seven U.S. Presidents were Left handed!
List of Recent U.S. Presidents

	President	Dates in office	Party	Handed
38th	Gerald Ford (1913–2006)	9/8/74 – 20/1/77	Republican	Left
39th	Jimmy Carter (1924–)	20/1/77 – 20/1/81	Democratic	Right
40th	Ronald Reagan (1911–2004)	20/1/81 – 20/1/89	Republican	Left
41th	George H. W. Bush (1924–)	20/1/89 – 20/1/93	Republican	Left
42th	Bill Clinton (1946–)	20/1/93 – 20/1/01	Democratic	Left

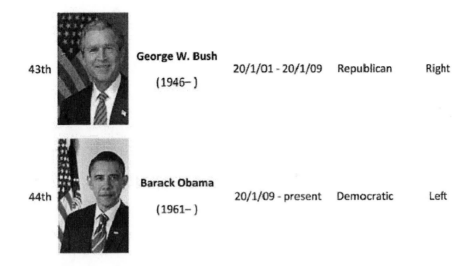

43th	**George W. Bush** (1946–)	20/1/01 - 20/1/09	Republican	Right
44th	**Barack Obama** (1961–)	20/1/09 - present	Democratic	Left

Being part of any minority means that you attract attention and usually means that other people are a little wary of you. The word "sinister" is sometimes used to refer to left handers and in ancient times it was seen as a sign of the devil.

In the last hundred years as full-time education became standard there has been a pressure on left handed people to change to use their right hands as this made things easier for the teacher. It was not unusual up to a quarter of a century ago to tie a child's left hand behind his or her back in order to encourage the use of the right hand.

Of course, in cases where one hand is injured it is necessary to develop the use of the other hand. Many people will remember Bob Dole, the American presidential candidate, who suffered a serious injury to his right hand whilst in combat and had to train himself to use his left hand in order to write. Most of us at some time will injure our preferred hand and, if only for a short time, have to learn to write with our non-preferred hand.

Chapter 10

CONCLUSION

This is a scientific book. It has been written by a team of experienced and highly qualified Human Movement Scientists in order to bring the latest, up-to-date knowledge on children's handedness to the people who need it most, the parents and teachers who are dealing with children on a daily basis. Time has been taken to explain any complex concepts and to make the book accessible to those who are likely to need to read it.

Human Movement Science is a relatively new academic subject at the junction of Biomechanics, Sports Science, Sports Coaching and Sports Psychology. The people working in the field are investigating the way that people, particularly young people, move and some of the problems that they have in moving well, such as in cases of Dyspraxia, Cerebral Palsy, Multiple Sclerosis, etc..

As with all science there is a need to take the science out of books, where it can do little good, and take it to the coalface, in this case, to the parents and teachers who are struggling with the problem of children with handedness problems.

This book grew out of the website of the Times Educational Supplement. The London *Times* is the first and, most well respected daily newspaper in the United Kingdom and contains the Court Circular of the daily plans for each of the senior members of the Royal Family. It is the newspaper of the establishment in the U.K. Its Educational Supplement is a weekly paper for those in the educational industry from kindergarten, primary, secondary to further and higher education. It is the voice of teachers in the U.K.

The T.E.S. website recently contained copies of over three hundred and fifty letters from young teachers in charge of reception classes at primary schools, those places where children aged between 4.5, 5 and 6 years go for their first days at school, where the children learn to live away from home, away from parents and siblings and to start living independent lives.

These letters were heartfelt pleas from highly trained young teachers who were doing their best and working very hard, but who were struggling with the problem of children's handedness. The letters told the story that for the last fifty years, almost since universal formal education had been introduced, teachers had been confident that young children attending school for the first days of their education, would know whether they were right or left handed and would be happy to start scribbling, coloring, tracing, drawing and writing as soon as they were given a crayon, pencil or pen.

Suddenly, and without warning, at the start on the new academic year in September 2008, many of these teachers had realized that many of the children had no idea how to hold a writing implement and worse still, which hand to hold it in. The teachers, who had never had to deal with this problem, had no strategy to deal with this problem and were desperately seeking advice. Unfortunately, none of their colleagues had experienced a similar problem, so none of them had any advice to give.

The authors were, at the time of becoming aware of this correspondence, completing a large scale research project on Dyspraxia and working with young children at primary schools. The issue of handedness was discussed with a number of senior teachers and managers and it was found that the number of children who were unaware of their handedness was approximately

25%, which interested the researchers as that is the number of children who are mixed handed.

The researchers determined that as soon as they completed their current study, then would start looking into handedness and try to help the teachers.

The research

Having already read the letters, spoken to the class teachers and their senior colleagues, and established the scope of the problem, the next stage was to explore the science and find out what was already known about the subject. Clearly, handedness has fascinated scientists for many years and there were large quantities of research papers that needed to be read, but no trace could be found of anybody trying to find a way of identifying whether a young child was right or left handed because the problem had never been identified. Children had always turned up at school knowing which hand they preferred to use.

Looking at the other books already available showed that thousands of books have been written on the subject of handedness and these have frequently been written by those parents and teachers who have experience of dealing with children with handedness issues. This experience is of unquestioned value, but it does mean that the books are practical rather than theoretical. There appeared to be a need for a book based on the current science.

A team of eight Human Movement Scientists applied their minds to the problem of designing a suitable test or series of tests to identify whether a child is right handed, left handed or mixed handed. It quickly became clear that this was not a simple question and that most children had to make a series of decisions on handedness for different tasks and that a child who wrote with his or her right hand may kick a football with his or her left foot.

These tests would have to be simple and easy to undertake by teachers in a classroom setting. Authority was then secured to conduct the research from the Local Authorities in Croydon in South London and in Edinburgh, Scotland. As Scottish schools start back in August and English schools start back in September, this permitted a large number of children to be tested on their first days at school before they had been "corrupted" by teachers and any influence brought to bear on them to change their hand preference.

So what had changed to cause this new problem?

Social Factors

We are constantly hearing of the long hours and commitment that is required today in order to achieve a successful lifestyle. We read in the press about "Superwomen" who are wives and mothers able to hold down a job earning £1M a year as well as managing a family. But can anybody really maintain the standards that are required to achieve this both at home and at work or is it that as well as these woman are doing, some things are getting past them?

There is an anecdote in the book about a child with a cut head, whose mother failed to see the injury in the four hours that they spent together after school. This shows that things are not as good as they should be and that children are missing out on the care and attention that they need to grow and develop. The mother had completed a day at the office and satisfied her employers. She had made it home in time to collect the child and to go shopping and made dinner. The mother and child has spent time together, but she had never looked him in the face or she would have seen the terrible cut.

A child's lifestyle today

A child's lifestyle today is completely different than it has ever been before. A perception of danger means that most parents keep their children at home when they feel that they can be protected and kept safe. The parents, however, have a long list or business and family commitments and so do not have time to engage with the children. The only solution is to allow the child to use the technology available to entertain him or herself. Television, video, computers, mobile phones, email, etc. keep the children safe and quiet.

At bedtime these children are sent to a bedroom full of the same technology. Who would want to go to sleep when there are interesting programs on television or you can watch videos or email, text or call friends for a chat. When these children are called to breakfast it is difficult to get them to respond, probably because they have not yet been to sleep and are ready to start now.

The old fashioned child's lifestyle

The first author grew up half a century ago on the southern fringes of London. His father worked in the City of London and left for work at 8.00

a.m. sharp every morning. A few minutes later the child would be given breakfast and sent out to play in the surrounding fields with two rounds of sandwiches, an apple and an orange and a bottle of very weak orange squash to last the day and told not to return until 6.00 p.m., when his father returned from work.

The day was spent socializing with friends, chasing them around the fields and engaging with nature by chasing cows and sheep and using nets to catch frogs, lizards, snakes and butterflies, etc. The children did not stop exercising as they ran, climbed, wrestled, chased, etc. all day. They got very fit, learned to socialize, learned about the environment and eat healthily.

Aren't the lifestyle changes essential?

Today, many parents would point out the dangers associated with allowing young people to go out unsupervised, but dangers have always existed. The area described above, where the author lived, had no less than twelve mental hospitals within a six mile radius of his home and the patients were employed as dustbin men and street cleaners as part of their recovery program. The children were taught how to deal with potential danger.

As children start to grow they need vast quantities of vigorous exercise, appropriate to their age and stage of development. Ideally this exercise should be undertaken not in the house, or even at school or at the gym, but in a natural wilderness where they can run wild, climb trees and wrestle with their friends under the caring eye of a parent. Research has shown that exercise in this environment results in a doubling of the improvements in fitness and also leads to academic and intellectual benefits. It also leads the child to want to sleep at night.

A child put to bed in a room with nothing but a bed, will quickly get bored and fall asleep. If he or she has exercised vigorously, this is guaranteed. Parents may also be reassured that their children are not studying terrorism, drugs, sex or other subjects of which they do not approve.

Good, old fashioned food, avoiding the processed sweets and fizzy drinks that are supercharged with fats and sugars, combined with vigorous exercise, means that children can eat large quantities of food without fear of obesity.

Child development

Children are born weak and feeble and if left unattended in the first few weeks of life will die very quickly. As any parent will explain, babies require constant care and attention both night and day in order to thrive. In order to grow they need regular supplies of food and drink.

They need to be washed, their clothes need cleaning and they need changing. As they get older they need social contact to stimulate them, they need games to play to arouse them intellectually and to encourage exercise to build their fitness levels and their muscles. The pictures on television of children in Rumanian orphanages who had been left without social or intellectual stimulation must frighten any parent.

Children are in many ways like inflatable dolls, they require pumping up with food and drink to survive and help them grow. They need love and attention and exercise and intellectual challenges to develop. It is all about what you put in and what you get out.

Antiques programs on television show outstanding examples of manual skills of young people that have been forgotten in recent years. Samplers, containing wonderful embroidery produced by every teenage girl, carpentry and handwriting produced by every boy, depending on his academic achievement. They have been replaced by keyboarding skills and texting. But whilst computers are largely symmetrical, children are not and their development is suffering, particularly in areas such as handedness.

The solution?

This book has been written by scientists who have read all the available research on the subject and then spent several months working with a couple of hundred children in London and Edinburgh, testing their skills.

This book has been designed to set out the facts that parents and teachers need in order to understand the importance of handedness and the facts as they are currently known to be. Then a few games are introduced to allow the adult and child to explore the child's skills at the same time as bonding together. Later, a few detailed tests are introduced to assist in a full investigation of the child's skills.

This is followed by a range of exercises which will assist any child who has been found to lack any of the manual skills. Finally, there is a section which is designed to assist children to come to terms with their test results by listing some of the people who are left handed or mixed handed and who have achieved success in their chosen fields of activity.

Many previous books have focused on children who are left handed and clearly, these are the children who have historically always been seen as the problem. It is very simple to see a continuum in which most children are right handed, some are not sure and sit between right handed and left handed and a few are clearly left handed. This has been shown in this book not to be the case.

In fact, the research has shown that children with a strong hand preference, whether it be for the right or left hand, are very close in the way that their brains work. The children who are exceptional are those who are mixed handed and who have no strong hand preference. They have symmetrical brains, which are wired in a substantially different way than the children with strong hand preferences. For this reason it is these children who need particular attention and support.

This book will have been a success if it assists teachers to identify whether each of their students is right handed, left handed or mixed handed and assisted them to deal with the situations in which these decisions place them.

REFERENCES

Annett, M. & Kilshaw, D. (1983). Right- and left-hand skill II: Estimating the parameters of the distribution of L-R differences in males and females. *British Journal of Psychology.* 74 (2), 269–283.

Annett, M. & Kilshaw, D. (1984). Lateral preference and skill in dyslexics: Implications of the right shift theory. *Journal of Child Psychology and Psychiatry.* 25(3), 357-377.

Annett, M. & Manning, M. (1990). Arithmetic and laterality. *Neuropsychologia.* 28(1), 61-69.

Annett, M. & Turner, A. (1974). Laterality and the Growth of Intellectual Abilities. *British Journal of Educational Psychology.* 44 (1), pages 37–46.

Annett, M. (1964). A Model of the Inheritance of Handedness and Cerebral Dominance *Nature* 204, 59-60.

Annett, M. (1970)a. A Classification of Hand Preference by Association Analysis. *British Journal of Psychology.* 61, (3) 303–321.

Annett. M. (1970)b, The growth of manual preference and speed. *British Journal of Psychology*, 61, 545-558.

Annett, M. (1972). The Distribution of Manual Asymmetry. *British Journal of Psychology.* 63 (3) 343–358.

Annett, M. (1978). Throwing loaded and unloaded dice. *Behavioral and Brain Sciences*, 1, 278-279.

Annett (1995). The right shift theory of a gentics balanced polymorphism for cerebral dominance and cognitive processing, *Current Psychology of Cognition.* 14, 427-480.

Annett, M. (2001). *Handedness and Brain Asymmetry: The Right Shift Theory.* Sussex: Psychology Press. ISBN-13: 978-1841691046.

Ayres, A.J. (1978). Southern California sensory-motor integration tests manual, CA: Western Psychological Services.

Azemar, G. (1993). Les gauchers en excrime: Donnees, statistique et interpretation, *Escrime Internationale*, 7, 15-19.

Ballard, P.B. (1912). What London children like to draw, *Journal of Experimental Pediatrics,* 3,. 185-197;

Benbow, C.P. (1986). Physiological correlates of extreme intellectual precocity. *Neuropsychologia.*24, (5) 719-725.

Berger, S.E., Friedman, R. & Polis, M.S. (2011). The role of locomotor posture and experience on handedness and footedness in infancy. *Infant Behavior and Development.* 34(3) 472-480.

Berk, L.E. (2008). Child Development. MA: Pearson Education. ISBN-13: 978-0205507061.

Birtles, D., Anker, S., Atkinson, J., Shellens, R., Briscoe, A., Mahoney, M. & Braddick, O. (2011). Bimanual strategies for object retrieval in infants and young children. *Experimental Brain Research.* 211(2) 207-218.

Bishop, D.V.M. (1990). *Handedness and developmental disorder.* London: Mac Keith Press. ISBN-13: 978-0397480197

Bolser, L.A., Runfeldt, S., Morris, R.A. (1988). Handedness in language – trained chimpanzee in daily activities and assessment tasks, *Journal of Clinical and Experimental Neuropsychology*, 10, 40-41.

Brewster, E.T. (1913). The ways of the left hand. *McClure's Mag.* 41, 168-183.

Bryden, M. P, Hécaen, H. & DeAgostini, M. (1983). Patterns of cerebral organization. *Brain and Language*, 20(2), 249-262.

Bryden, M.P., Hecaen, H., & deAgostini, M. (1982). Patterns of cerebral organization, University of Waterloo, Waterloo, Ontarion, Mimeo.

Bryden, P.J., Pryde, K.M. & Roy, E.A (2000). A developmental analysis of the relationship between hand preference and performance: II. A performance-based method of measuring hand preference in children. Brain and Cognition, 43(1-3), 60-64.

Bryngelson, B. (1939). A Study of Laterality of Stutterers and Normal Speakers. *Journal of Speech and Hearing Disorders.*4, 231-234.

Byrne, B. (1974). Handedness and musical ability. *British Journal of Psychology*, 65(2), 279-281.

Byrne, R.W. and Byrne, J.M. (1991). Hand preferences in the skilled gathering tasks of mountain gorillas. *Cortex*, 27, 521-546.

Chambers, M. & Sugden, D. (2006). *Early Years Movement Skills: Description, Diagnosis and Intervention* London: Wiley-Blackwell. ISBN-13: 978-1861564986

Chen, W.J. & Su, C.H. (2006). Handedness and schizotypy in non-clinical populations: Influence of handedness measures and age on the relationship Laterality: Asymmetries of Body, Brain, and Cognition, 11 (4) 331-349.

Chodhari, R. Mitchison, M. & Meeks, M. (2004). Cilia, primary ciliary dyskinesia and molecular genetics. *Paediatric Respiratory Reviews.* 5 (1), 69-76.

Cole, J. (1955). Paw preference in cats related to hand preference in animals and men. *Journal of Comparative and Physiological Psychology*, 48(2), 137-140.

Collins, R.L. (1969.) On the Inheritance of Handedness. *Journal of Heredity*. 60 (3): 117-119.

Connolly, K., & Elliot, J. (1972). The evolution of and ontogeny of hand function. IN N. Blurton Jones (Ed.), Ethological studies of child behaviour. London and New York: Cambridge Univ. Press.

Corballis, M.C., Hattie, J. & Fletcher, R. (2008). Handedness and intellectual achievement: An even-handed look. Neuropsychologia. 46(1) 374-378.

Corbetta, D., Williams, J. and Snapp-Childs, W. (2006), Plasticity in the development of handedness: Evidence from normal development and early asymmetric brain injury. *Developmental Psychobiology*, 48: 460–471.

Coren, S. (1990). Left Handedness: Behavioural Implications and Anomalies Amsterdam, Netherlands: Elsevier Science Ltd. ISBN-13: 978-0444884381.

Coren, S., Porac, C., & Duncan, P. (1981). Lateral preference behaviors in preschool children and young adults, *Child Development*, 52 (2) 443-450.

Craig, J.D. (1980). A dichotic rhythm task: Advantage for the left-handed. *Cortex*. 16(4) 613-20.

Crow, T.J. (2004). Cerebral asymmetry and the lateralization of language: core deficits in schizophrenia as pointers to the gene. *Current Opinion in Psychiatry*. 17(2) 97-106.

Crow, T.J., Crow, L.R., Done, D.J. & Leask, S. (1998). Relative hand skill predicts academic ability: global deficits at the point of hemispheric indecision. *Neuropsychologia* 36 (12) 1275-1282.

Darwin, C. (1859) *The Origin of Species* Ware, Herts: Wordsworth Editions Ltd. ISBN-13: 978-1853267802

De Agostini, M., Khamis, A.H., Ahui, A.M. & Dellatolas, G. (1997). Environmental influences in hand preference: An African point of view. *Brain and Cognition*. 35(2) 151-167.

de Kay, J.T. (1998). Left-handed Kids London: Robson Books Ltd. ISBN-13: 978-1861051141.

Deutsch, D. (1980). Handedness and memory for total pitch. IN J. Herron (1980). Neuropsychology of Left-handedness: Perspectives in Neurolinguistics and Psycholinguistics. NY: Academic Press Inc. ISBN-13: 978-0123431509.

Elliott, D. (1985). Manual asymmetries in the performance of sequential movement by adolescents and adults with Down syndrome. *American Journal of Mental Deficiency*, 90(1), 90-97.

Ellis, S.J., Ellis, P.J. & Marshall, E. (1988). Hand preference in a normal population. Cortex: 24(1) 157-163

Fagan, L.B. (1931). The relation of dextral training to the onset of stuttering, A report of cases, Quarterly Journal of Speech, 17, 73-76.

Fagot, J. & Vauclair, J. (1988). Handedness and bimanual coordination in the lowland gorilla. *Brain, Behavior and Evolution*, 32(2), 89-95

Fein, G.G. (1986). The affective psychology of play. In A. W. Gottfried & C. C. Brown (Eds.), *Play interactions: The contributions of play material and parental involvement to children's development.* Lexington, MA: Lexington Books.

Ferre, C.L., Babik, I. & Michel, G.F. (2010). Development of infant prehension handedness: A longitudinal analysis during the 6- to 14-month age period. *Infant Behavior and Development. 33(4)* 492-502.

Finch, G. (1941). Chimpanzee handedness. *Science*, 94, 117-118.

Fischer, R.B., Meunier, G.F. & White, P.J. (1982). Evidence of laterality in the lowland gorilla. *Perceptual and Motor Skills*, 54(3), 1093-1094.

Francks, C., Maegawa, S., Laurén, J., Abrahams, B.S., Velayos-Baeza, A., Medland, S.E., Colella, S., Groszer, M., McAuley, E.Z., Caffrey, T.M., Timmusk, T., Pruunsild, P., Koppel, I., Lind, P.A., Matsumoto-Itaba, N., Nicod, J., Xiong, L., Joober, R., Enard, W., Krinsky, B., Nanba, E., Richardson, A.J., Riley, B.P., Martin, N.G., Strittmatter, S.M., Möller, H.-J., Rujescu, D., St Clair, D., Muglia, P., Roos, J.L., Fisher, S.E., Wade-Martins, R., Rouleau, G.A., Stein, J.F., Karayiorgou, M., Geschwind, D.H., Ragoussis, J., Kendler, K.S., Airaksinen, M.S., Oshimura, M., DeLisi, L.E., & Monaco, A. P. (2007).LRRTM1 on chromosome 2p12 is a maternally suppressed gene that is associated paternally with handedness and schizophrenia. Molecular Psychiatry,12, 1129-1139.

Gesell, A. & Ames, L.B. (1947). The development of handedness. *The Pedagogical Seminary and Journal of Genetic Psychology*, 70, 155-175.

Gillberg, C., Waldenström, E. and Rasmussen, P. (1984), Handedness in Swedish 10-year-olds. Some Background and Associated Factors. *Journal of Child Psychology and Psychiatry*, 25: 421–432.

Goodall, J. (1986). The chimpanzee of the Gombe stream reserve, <u>IN DeVore, I.</u> (1965). Primate Behaviour: Field Studies of Monkeys and Apes NY: Holt, Rinehart & Winston. ISBN-13: 978-0030503405

Gottfried, A.W. & Bathurst K (1983). Hand preference across time is related to intelligence in young girls, not boys. *Science221*, 1074-1076.

Grattan, M.P., de Vos, E., Levy, J. & McClintock, M.K. (1992). Asymmetric action in the human newborn: Sex differences in patterns of organization. *Child Development. 63(2)* 273–289.

Harris, L.J. (1980). Left handedness: Early theories, facts and fancies. IN J. Herron (1980). Neuropsychology of Left-handedness: Perspectives in Neurolinguistics and Psycholinguistics. NY: Academic Press Inc. ISBN-13: 978-0123431509.

Hecaen, H. & Ajuriaguerra, J.D. (1964). *Left-handedness: Manual Superiority and Cerebral Dominance* New York: Grune & Stratton. ISBN-13: 978-0808901853

Hinojosa, T., Sheu, C.F. & Michel, G.F. (2003). Infant hand-use preferences for grasping objects contributes to the development of a hand-use preference for manipulating objects. *Developmental Psychobiology. 43(4)* 328–334.

Iaccino, J.F. (1993*). Left Brain-Right Brain Differences: Inquiries, Evidence and New Approaches.* NY: Psychology Press. ISBN-13: 978-0805813418.

Jokl, E. (1981).Zu den neurologischen Grundlagen des Handelns. In: Lenk H. (Hrsg.) Handlungstheorien-interdisziplinär, Band.3:57-77.

Kanizsa, G. (1955). "Margini quasi-percettivi in campi con stimolazione omogenea.", *Rivista di Psicologia* 49 (1): 7–30.

Kilshaw, D. & Annett, M. (1983). Right- and left-hand skill I: Effects of age, sex and hand preference showing superior skill in left-handers *British Journal of Psychology.* 74, (2) 253–268.

Kim, D., Raine, A., Triphon, N. & Green, M.F. (1992). Mixed handedness and features of schizotypal personality in a nonclinical sample. *Journal of Nervous and Mental Disease*, 180(2), 133-135.

Lazarus, J.A., & Todor, .J.I. (1987). Age differences in the magnitude of associated movement. Developmental Medicine and Child Neurology. 29(6) 726-33.

Leask, S.J. & Crow, T.J. (1997). How far does the brain lateralize? an unbiased method for determining the optimum degree of hemispheric specialization. Neuropsychologia.; 35(10) 1381-7.

Lehman, R.A.W. (1987). On the other hand, Behavioral and Brain Sciences, 10, 280-281.

Lucas, J.A., Rosenstein, L.D. & Bigler, E.D. (1989). Handedness and language among the mentally retarded: Implications for the model of pathological left-handedness and gender differences in hemispheric specialization. *Neuropsychologia.* 27, (5) 713-723

MacNeilage, P.F., Studdert-Kennedy, M.G. & Lindblom, B. ((1987) Primate handedness reconsidered *Behavioral and Brain Sciences* 10: 247-263.

Major, D.R. (1906). First steps in mental growth; A series of studies in the psychology of infancy. London: Macmillan & Co. Ltd. ASIN: B00010IKI0I.

Marchant, L.F. & McGrew, W.C. (1996). Laterality of limb function in wild chimpanzees of Gombe National Park: comprehensive study of spontaneous activities *Journal of Human Evolution* 30(5), 427-443.

McManus, I.C. (1984). Genetics of handedness in relation to language disorder, *Advances in Neurology*, 42, 125-138.

Morley, M.E. (1957). *The Development and Disorders of Speech in Childhood. Edinburgh: E. & S.* Livingstone. ASIN: B0000CJOYQ.

Nalçaci, E., Kalaycioğlu, C., Çiçek, M. & Genç, Y. (2001).The Relationship between Handedness and Fine Motor Performance. *Cortex*. 37, 493-500

Nash-Wortham, M. & Hunt, J. (2003). Take Time: Movement Exercises for Parents, Teachers and Therapists of Children with Difficulties in Speaking, Reading, Writing and Spelling. Stourbridge: Robinswood Press. ISBN-13: 978-1869981587.

Obel, C., Hedegaard, M., Henriksen, T.B., Secher, N.J., & Olsen, J. (2003). Psychological factors in pregnancy and mixed-handedness in the offspring, *Developmental Medicine and Child Neurology*, 45(8) 557-561.

Orton, S.J. (1937). Reading, writing and speech problems in children. New York, N.Y. Norton ASIN B001AG1WAK. IN M. Annett, (2001). *Handedness and Brain Asymmetry: The Right Shift Theory.* Sussex: Psychology Press. ISBN-13: 978-1841691046.

Payne, M.A. (1987). Impact of cultural pressures on self-reports of actual and approved hand use. *Neuropsychologia*. 25(2) 247-258.

Pense, S. (2002). Paw Preference in Rats. *Journal of Basic and Clinical Physiology and Pharmacology.* 13, (1), 41-50.

Perelle, I.B. & Ehrman, L. (1994). An international study of human handedness: The data. *Behavior Genetics* 24(3) 217-227.

Perelle, I.B. and Ehrman, L. (1994). An international study of human handedness: The data. *Behavior Genetics* 24, (3), 217-227.

Petrie, B.F. & Peters, M. (1980). Handedness: Left/right differences in intensity of grasp response and duration of rattle holding in infants[*] *Infant Behavior and Development.* 3, 215-221.

Piek, J.P. (2006). *Infant Motor Development.* Champaign IL: Human Kinetics Publishers. ISBN-13: 978-0736002264

Pipe, M.E. (1987). Pathological left-handedness: Is it familial? *Neuropsychologia.* 25, (3) 571-577.

Porac, C. & Coren, S. (1981). *Lateral Preferences and Human Behavior.* London: Springer ISBN-13: 978-0387905969.

Poreh, A.M., Levin, J. Teves, H. & States, J. (1997). Mixed handedness and schizotypal personality in a non-clinical sample-The role of task demand. *Personality and Individual Differences.* 23, (3) 501-507.

Preti, A., Rocchi, M.B, Sisti, D., Mura, T., Manca, .S, Siddi, S., Petretto, D.R., Masala, C. (2007). The psychometric discriminative properties of the Peters et al Delusions Inventory: a receiver operating characteristic curve analysis. Comparative Psychiatry. 48(1)62-9.

Price, M. (2009). The left brain knows what the right hand is doing, *Monitor on Psychology*, 40 (1), 60.

Provins, K. A. (1997). Handedness and speech: A critical reappraisal of the role of genetic and environmental factors in the cerebral lateralization of function. *Psychological Review*, 104(3) 554-571.

Provins, K. A.; Milner, A.D. & Kerr, P. (1982). Asymmetry of manual preference and performance. *Perceptual and Motor Skills*, 54(1), 179-194.

Ramsay, D.S. (1980). Beginnings of bimanual handedness and speech in infants. *Infant Behavior and Development.* 3, 67-77.

Rogers, L.J. (2000). Evolution of Hemispheric Specialization: Advantages and Disadvantages. *Brain and Language. 73(2)* 236-253.

Rönnqvist, L. & Domellöf, E. (2006). Quantitative assessment of right and left reaching movements in infants: A longitudinal study from 6 to 36 months. *Developmental Psychobiology*, 48(6) 444–459.

Ronnqvist, L., & Hopkins, B. (1998). Head position preference in the human newborn: A new look, Child Development, 69, 13-23.

Schaller, G.B. (1963). The mountain gorilla: Ecology and behavior. Oxford, England: Chicago University Press. ASIN: B0000CLSDI.

Schmidt, R.A. & Wrisberg, C.A. (2004). Motor Learning and Performance. Champaign, IL: Human Kinetics Publishers. ISBN-13: 978-0736045667.

Searleman, A. & Fugagli, A.K. (1987). Suspected autoimmune disorders and left-handedness: Evidence from individuals with diabetes, Crohn's disease and ulcerative colitis. *Neuropsychologia.* 25(2) 367-374.

Shaw, J. Claridge, G. & Clark, K. (2001). Schizotypy and the shift from dextrality: a study of handedness in a large non-clinical sample *Schizophrenia Research* 50(3) 181-189.

Stadler, R., & Bucher, W. (Ed.) (1986).*Erfolg mit beiden Seiten.Die Tennistechnik mit Zukunft.* Dübendorf/Unterägeri.

Starosta, W. (2004). Types and effects of motor adaptation a left-handed persons in daily life and in contemporary sport training. Daphne, AL: Sport Journal.

Stroop, J. R. (1935). Studies of interference in serial verbal reactions. *Journal of Experimental Psychology, 12*, 643-662.

Szaflaraski, J.P., Binder, J.R., Possing, E.T., McKiernan, K.A. Ward, B.D. & Hammeke, T.A. (2002). Language lateralization in left-handed and ambidextrous people; fMRI data. *Neurology.* 59.(2) 238-244

Tapley, S.M. and Bryden, M.P. (1985). Neuropsychologica. 23: 215 -221.

Uzgiris, I.C. (1967). Ordinality in the development of schemas for relating to objects, In J. Hellmuth. (1971). *Exceptional infant.* London: Butterworth. ISBN-13: 978-0876300343.

Vargha-Khadem, F., O'Gorman, A.M., Watters, G.V. (1985) Aphasia and Handedness in Relation to Hemispheric side, Age at Injury and Severity of Cerebral Lesion during Childhood. *Brain* 108 (3): 677-696.

Vuoksimaa, E., Koskenvuo, M. Rose, R.J. & Kaprio, J. (2009). Origins of handedness: A nationwide study of 30 161 adults. *Neuropsychologia. 47(5)* 1294-1301.

Warren, J.M. (1980).Handedness and laterality in humans and other animals. *Physiological Psychology.* 8(3), 351-359.

Whitty, P., Clarke, M. McTigue, O., Browne, S. Gervin, M, Kamali, M. Lane, A. Kinsella, A. Waddington, J., Larkin, C. & O'Callaghan, E. (2006). Diagnostic specificity and predictors of neurological soft signs in schizophrenia, bipolar disorder and other psychoses over the first 4 years of illness. *Schizophrenia Research.* 86(1-3) 110-117.

Wile, I.S. (1934). Handedness: Right and Left. Boston: Lathrop, Lee and Shepherd. ASIN: B0018HQ56M.

Williams, H. G. (1983). *Perceptual and motor development.* Englewood Cliffs, N.J.: Prentice-Hall. ISBN 0136568920

Young, G., Segalowitz, S.J., Corter, C.M., & Trehub, S.E. (1983). *Manual specialization and the developing brain*, London: Academic Press.

Zhu, J.L., Obel, C., Basso, O., Bech, B.H., Henriksen, T.B., Olsen, J. (2009). Infertility, infertility treatment, and mixed-handedness in children *Early Human Development.* 85 (12) 745-749.

SCORE SHEET

Activity	Session 1		Session 2		Session 3		Session 4	
	Right	Left	Right	Left	Right	Left	Right	Left
Coin Games								
Playing Cards								

DOTTY PAPER (1)

DOTTY PAPER (2)

BALLOONS

IT'S RAINING (1)

IT'S RAINING (2)

TRIANGLE TREES

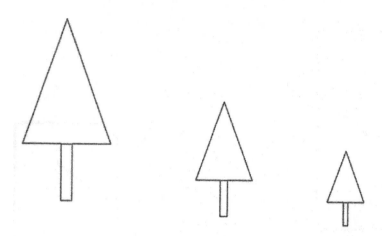

CHRISTMAS TREES

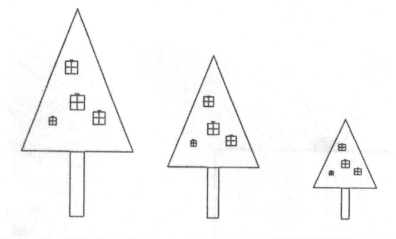

INSTRUMENTATION REQUIRED FOR THE WATHAND BOX TEST

The screwdriver, the hammer and the workbench

These are all part of the Peterkin Tool Carrycase ASIN: B000RPC4IY. Price $40.15 (U.S.A.) £8.99 (U.K.)
Available from Amazon.com

The Tool Carrycase also contains:

- 1 x Plastic carrycase
- 1 x Workbench top
- 2 x Workbench legs
- 1 x Saw
- 1 x Square (T rule)
- 1 x Wrench
- 1 x Hammer
- 1 x Screwdriver
- 2 x Nuts
- 2 x Bolts
- 2 x Pegs

The Toy with Small Buttons

Fisher-Price brilliant basics friendly flip phone ASIN: B000LSZVLO. Price $20.00 (U.S.A.) £20.00 (U.K.)
Available from Amazon.com

Tossing a Ball at a Target

This is a Velcro Ball and Catch ASIN: B001G4MVR4. Price $7.64 (U.S.A.) £4.59 (U.K.).
Available from Amazon.com

Round Cup Hook - Zinc Plated – 1 in/ 25mm

U.S.	U.K.
Model # 53564	Product no. 913964
$3.61 for 2-Pack	£1.79 for 4 Pack
Available from Home Depot	Available from Homebase

Rings - Steel Washers - M10 –

U.S.	U.K.
Model 32722	Product no. 564988
$3.37 for 25 Pack	£2.49 for 15 Pack
Available from Home Depot	Available from Homebase

Lock with Key

Masterlock Solid Brass Padlock - 40mm

U.S.	U.K.
Model # 141DLFHC	Product no. 635633
Available from Home Depot	£3.48
	Available from Homebase

Cupboard Door

Akran lockable cabinet £19.99 (U.K.)

U.S.	U.K.
Model # 166760	Product no. 245.865.10 (catalogue p195)
$29.99	£19.99
Available from Home Depot	Available from Ikea

INDEX

D

E

F